BEST OF IRISH
MEAT RECIPES

DELICIOUS MODERN RECIPES

Best of
Irish

BASED ON TRADITIONAL IRISH COOKING

BIDDY WHITE LENNON is a founder member and former Chairwoman of the Irish Food Writers Guild. She is the author of several cookbooks, including four previous titles in the *Best of Irish* series: *Potato Recipes, Traditional Cooking, Home Baking* and *Festive Cooking*. She has written and presented a ten-part television series on healthy eating for the Irish Department of Health.

Biddy writes about food and cooking for the *Irish Farmers' Journal*, gives talks and cookery demonstrations all over Ireland and is consulted about food and cooking by producers and retailers. As a freelance journalist she contributes to many publications, including *Food & Wine Magazine*. She is a regular broadcaster on television and radio on subjects as varied as health, social welfare, fashion, interiors and travel.

As an actress, she is perhaps best known in Ireland for her portrayal of Maggie in the hugely popular RTÉ television series, *The Riordans*, a role she played for fifteen years. She continued to act in the series when it moved to radio and also co-wrote many episodes with her husband, later writing for the TV series *Glenroe*.

Best of
Irish
Meat
RECIPES

BIDDY WHITE LENNON

THE O'BRIEN PRESS
DUBLIN

First published 2006 by The O'Brien Press Ltd,
12 Terenure Road East, Rathgar, Dublin 6, Ireland.
Tel: +353 1 4923333; Fax: +353 1 4922777
E-mail: books@obrien.ie
Website: www.obrien.ie

ISBN-10: 0-86278-931-1
ISBN-13: 978-0-86278-931-2

British Library Cataloguing-in-Publication Data
White Lennon, Biddy
Best of Irish meat recipes
1.Cookery (Meat) 2.Cookery, Irish
I.Title II.Stampton, Tim
641.6'6'09415

1 2 3 4 5 6 7
06 07 08 09 10

Editing, layout, typesetting, design: The O'Brien Press Ltd
Author photograph: Denis Latimer
Internal illustrations: Tim Stampton
Cover photography: Walter Pfeiffer
Printing: Cox & Wyman Ltd

Contents

Introduction

Geography, geology, the history of our different peoples down thousands of years and, most of all, the temperate climate of the island have all contributed to an Irish food culture that places an emphasis on meat and poultry.

The first thing visitors notice when they arrive in Ireland is how green it is. Now, on relatively rare sunny days, we avoid telling them it's rain that makes Ireland green. But it is the green, green grass our animals graze on for most of the year, living naturally in our fields, on our hillsides and mountainsides that makes Irish meat so good to eat. Meat has been central to Irish food culture for thousands of years. Long before the Celts arrived we were a meat-loving people eating a wide variety of animals, furred and feathered wild game, as well as domesticated animals like goat, sheep, cattle and pigs. The Celts, however, valued cattle above all other animals. A pastoral system of farming emerged and the herding and protection of cattle from animal and human predators was a fulltime occupation.

Neolithic farmers had already introduced the domesticated pig to supplement the meat of the native wild boar. These pigs were allowed to run fairly wild and were noted for their height, pugnacity and fitness. They were fertile, too, expected to rear a litter of nine piglets in their first year. A prosperous man was expected to keep two breeding sows and have a bronze cauldron large enough to boil a boar, which was always served at feasts. The king received the leg and his queen the haunch; the head of the boar went to the charioteer.

The arrival of the Normans brought more advanced agricultural methods, placed great emphasis on sheep and introduced new breeds of both domesticated and game animals and birds. By early Norman times the wild boar had been hunted almost to extinction and the domesticated pig assumed its crucial place in the life of the native Irish. In the sixteenth century, the Normans – now known as 'old English' and judged by the Tudor rulers of England to have become 'more Irish than the Irish' – and the native Irish were replaced by the 'new English' in a massive transfer of lands known as 'the plantations'. Agricultural practice changed again. For a century or so most of the land was under pasture, rearing huge herds of cattle and sheep for export. A further series of plantations under the Stuart rulers of the combined kingdoms of Scotland and England saw many Scottish planters taking over land, particularly in the northern part of the island.

The native Irish, by now existing on tiny smallholdings, depended on pork and bacon from the family pig to provide what small quantities of meat they got to eat. Their ingenuity in curing (salting) and spicing pig meat far outstripped their use of sheep meat, beef, wild game and fowl.

Two distinct food cultures emerged. Elaborate meals were served in the 'big houses', which were well supplied with meat, farmyard fowl and game and had cold-store rooms, elaborate facilities for cooking and the money to employ trained cooks and servants. Peter Somerville-Large in his book *Dublin* (Hamish Hamilton, 1979) tells of a Mrs Delany who, when serving a first course 'might include turkey, endive, plum pudding, venison pasty and roast loin of veal, to be followed by a second course consisting of partridge, collared pig, crabs, creamed apple-tarts and pigeons'.

For the overwhelming majority who lived in cabins and cottages and whose cooking facilities were a turf-fuelled open fire and a hearth wide enough for smoking meat, meals were simple and often limited to what they could rear or gather from the wild; death or transportation awaited those who got caught poaching.

The rich food culture of the Gaelic-speaking native Irish, which was based on beef and milk, withered, but simple one-pot dishes flavoured with wild herbs, fruit and nuts survived. So too did the traditional craft of curing and smoking and, for those who could afford it, spicing meat.

Caught in the middle were the 'strong' tenant farmers who could afford to keep back some cattle, sheep and pigs for the house. They took pride in keeping up the ancient tradition of hospitality by giving less fortunate neighbours gifts of fresh meat and fowl on festive occasions. Their women-folk cultivated a 'kitchen garden' (really only a vegetable and herb patch) and also reared substantial numbers of farmyard fowl which provided profits to spend on luxuries like imported spices, wines and dried fruit, at the town markets established in Norman times. Traditionally, there are two Irish approaches to cooking meat:

wet-cooked and dry-cooked. In wet cooking we slowly simmer both fresh and cured meats until tender in liquid that has been flavoured with 'pot herbs' which include root vegetables as well as leafy herbs. In dry cooking (roasting, grilling or frying), the food is cooked quickly and usually accompanied by potatoes and vegetables cooked separately. Even today, 'throwing together' a stew and setting it to simmer in a low oven for a few hours comes naturally to all but the very young, who, alas, now favour fast food.

Popular wet-cooked dishes include corned beef, boiled bacon and cabbage, tripe and onions, beef and stout stew, pork and cider stew, and stewed lamb with capers. Another type of wet cooking is pot-roasting, often used for meat, fowl and game that is past the first flush of youth. The meat is laid on a bed of sliced onions, leek, carrot and celery, allowing the juices they produce to make the dish moist when it is roasted slowly in a covered pot in the oven.

Despite what many visitors may have been led to believe, there is more to our dry-cooking repertoire than 'the full Irish' breakfast – a dish composed of fried bacon rashers, sausages, puddings, eggs, mushrooms and tomatoes. We grill or sear in a pan tender cuts of meat like beef steaks, chops, liver, pork fillets, prime cuts of venison, chicken and duck and then deglaze the pan with cider, or wine, or whiskey (with or without the addition of cream) to make a sauce. We roast meats, too, often flavouring them with the herbs used in Ireland since ancient times on which our grass-fed animals graze: wild thyme, marjoram, mint, sage, wild garlic leaves (ramsoms) and mustard seeds. We also use herbs introduced relatively recently, like rosemary, basil and tarragon. Traditionally roasts are accompanied by hot, spicy condiments like horseradish or mustard, or by fruity ones like the sauces and jellies made from native fruits: apples, rowan berries, elderberries and fraughans (blueberries). Meat, when eaten cold, is accompanied by chutneys and pickles made from fruits and vegetables. Bread or potato stuffings flavoured with onions, herbs, nuts and dried fruit are commonly served with pork, lamb, farmyard fowl and game birds.

We rarely abandon a favourite food. Every race that has settled or invaded the island has left its mark on our modern food culture. We have always taken what we liked and made it subtly our own. In that we are no different from other European countries. Nor are we different when we put our own spin on history. After Ireland regained independence, after a gap of about 700 years, there was a tendency to glorify the native Irish way of life and dismiss centuries of outside influences as 'not really Irish'. It makes no sense to try to suppress or selectively dismiss any of the influences that have made Irish culture, including our food culture, what it is today.

As a result of immigration, Ireland is rapidly becoming more multicultural and we have restaurants and food shops all over the island specialising in Italian, French, Spanish, Chinese, Indian, African and eastern European foods. An expanding number of artisan and speciality food producers now make European speciality foods as well as traditional Irish products and sell them at farmers' markets, which are not unlike the fairs and markets of Norman Ireland. There is, rightly, a new pride in Irish food traditions and, happily, our chefs (who were once taught to value French classic cooking above all else) have become interested in exploring and learning about their own food culture. Leading Irish chefs now take great pride in putting their individual 'contemporary spin' on traditional Irish dishes.

The recipes in this book are laid out in six sections: fresh beef, fresh lamb, fresh pork, fresh poultry, game, and dishes using cured, spiced and smoked meats.

Beef

Our moist, temperate climate keeps the grass growing so that for most of the year Irish beef is largely grass-fed fresh in the fields, or fed silage made from the grass for the very few months of the year they are indoors.

Our appreciation of the value of cattle goes back a long way. Six thousand years ago hunting and gathering gave way to farming. The first farmers brought small cattle to Ireland. When, about two thousand six hundred years ago, the Celts began to arrive, the stage was set for the development of the Celtic cattle culture. The Celtic way of life depended on cattle in every way. A person's social standing and worth was reckoned in cattle – a free man or a woman was worth six heifers, or two milch cows, the unfree (slaves) were worth considerably less. Pagan religious festivals centred around cattle and the need to protect them. Cattle raiding was the national pastime and inspired heroic tales like the *Táin Bó Cuailnge*. Even in more recent times folklore records the length to which people went to protect their cattle from humans or people from the otherworld.

The native Irish were more interested in the food that could be produced from the milk than in the flesh itself. As a 'planter' in Tudor times complained, 'they will not kill a cow except it be old and yield no milk'.

As long as Celtic pastoral farming persisted the herds were brought together at the end of the grazing season and only beasts fit for breeding were spared from slaughter. Most animals were salted for winter use but some provided food for a feast for the extended family. Long after foreign farming methods were forced on the Irish, the custom of sharing the very best of what you had with your guests and neighbours survived, even in the harshest times. When they had beef, 'strong' farmers sent joints to less fortunate neighbours, particularly at festive times like Christmas.

Today, as in Celtic times, the Irish dairy industry dictates that the main source of male calves for beef production is from the dairy herd. Ireland exports vast quantities of beef to markets with differing demands. As a result, two main types of beef cattle exist: lean, late-maturing beef bred from continental sires (Limousin, Simmental, Charolais and Blonde d'Aquitaine) and early-maturing beef well-marbled with fat (and so much tastier) bred from Hereford, Angus and Shorthorn sires. The most highly regarded beef breeds are the Irish Angus and the Irish Hereford. The Hereford was introduced in 1775 and farmers quickly recognised the good sense of using a Hereford sire on Holstein cattle (the main dairy breed); the red, well-marbled flesh is very much to Irish taste. To this day, eighty per cent of craft butcher kills are Hereford or Hereford crosses. The same good eating quality applies to Angus, a breed that has grown in popularity in the last forty or so years.

OXTAIL STEW

In traditional craft butcher shops you will often see a bunch of meaty bones chopped into two- to three-inch pieces and tied together neatly in a round. They may look unpromising but, cooked with traditional Irish pot herbs, onion, carrot and celery, oxtails make the most delicious stew, or soup, provided you have time to wait – it needs four hours' gentle cooking and even then is at its best reheated the next day.

SERVES 4–6

Ingredients:

2 oxtails

2–3 carrots, peeled and chopped

2–3 onions, peeled and chopped

2–3 stick of celery, peeled and chopped

2–3 large tomatoes, or 2–3 tablesp tomato purée (optional)

2 bay leaves

1 teasp Irish wholegrain mustard

1 tablesp fresh marjoram or thyme

300 ml/10 fl oz red wine or stout

beef stock, enough to cover

salt and freshly ground black pepper

Method:

Trim away any larger pieces of fat. Clean the oxtail pieces in running water. Place in a pot with the vegetables, herbs, mustard, salt and pepper and add enough stock or water to cover. Bring slowly to simmering point, skim off any scum that rises to the surface. Add red wine or stout. Reduce to simmering point, cover, and cook very gently for 3–4 hours, or until the meat is falling off the bone. This can be done on the hob or in an oven set to 130°C/250°F/Gas ½. Allow to cool and then place in the fridge overnight. The next day remove any solid fat set on top and reheat slowly over a gentle heat in a pot or in the oven. Serve with root vegetables and steamed floury potatoes.

SOUP: Leftovers (or the whole dish) can be turned into oxtail soup, wonderfully warming and sustaining on a winter's day. When you have removed the fat from the top of the stew pick out the pieces of meat. Purée the vegetables and liquid together, pour back into a pot and reheat gently. Meanwhile remove bones and any fatty pieces from the oxtail pieces and return them to the pot to heat up with the liquid. If the soup is too thick add more water or stock.

TRIPE AND ONIONS

Tripe is the stomach tissue of cud-chewing animals, usually beef but sometimes veal (the best). Butchers sell it as 'dressed' tripe, which means it has been thoroughly cleaned and given a long initial cooking to tenderise it. The honeycomb-patterned tripe of the second stomach is tenderer than the flat or ridged variety of the first stomach. Dressed tripe still requires a couple of extra hours slow-cooking. Tripes à la mode de Caen is one of the great peasant dishes of Normandy in France. Is it unreasonable to believe that our love of tripe (cooked here with milk and onions, two very Irish ingredients) is something the Normans brought to Ireland and which we then took over?

SERVES 2–4 depending on appetite and need

Ingredients:

450 g/1 lb dressed honeycomb tripe

450 g/1 lb onions (peeled, chopped)

450 ml/15 fl oz milk

a pinch of grated nutmeg

salt and freshly ground black pepper

1 teasp cornflour

4 tablesp cream

2 tablesp fresh parsley, chopped

Method:

Cut the tripe into small 2 cm (1 inch) squares and bring to the boil in water. Drain. Place in a suitable baking dish or casserole along with the onions, milk (use just enough to cover), nutmeg and seasoning. Cook covered at 160°C /325°F/Gas 3 for at least 2 hours, or until completely tender. Use any remaining milk to top up the liquid if it gets too dry. About 10 minutes before serving, remove the lid and add the cornflour (which should be mixed in 2 tablespoons of water) and stir it in over a low heat until the sauce thickens. Add the cream and the chopped parsley; return briefly to the oven to heat through (do not boil) before serving with wholemeal bread.

FILLET OF BEEF WITH A BABY ONION SAUCE

This recipe was created by Sebastien Masi (head chef at the Pearl Brasserie in Dublin) for an Irish Food Writers Guild Good Food Awards luncheon.

SERVES 4

Ingredients:

4 x 200 g/7 oz fillets of beef

celery salt and freshly ground black pepper

2 shallots, peeled and finely chopped

150 g/5 oz baby silverskin onions (not pickled), halved

1 tablesp honey

1 tablesp water

125 ml/4 fl oz red wine

500 ml/16 fl oz veal, or chicken, stock

1 tablesp olive oil

about 30 g/1 oz butter

Method:

Make the sauce by cooking the baby onions and shallots gently in the honey and water in a small pan for about 20–30 minutes until caramelised; stir frequently. Deglaze the pan with the red wine, allowing it to bubble up well. Add stock and cook until the quantity of liquid has reduced by about one-third. Season to taste. Immediately before serving the sauce stir in a knob of butter to add a gloss.

Season the beef fillets with celery salt and coarsely ground black pepper. Preheat a heavy pan. When really hot add oil and a little butter and pan-fry the fillets for 4–5 minutes on each side (or for  more or less time depending on how you like your steak cooked). Rest in a warm place for five minutes before serving with the baby onion sauce.

SIRLOIN STEAK WITH WHISKEY AND CREAM SAUCE

You'll always find steak, in one guise or another, on every Irish menu and it is just as regularly served in every Irish home. This is a favourite recipe that works particularly well served with another favourite accompaniment – pan-fried mushrooms.

SERVES 4

Ingredients:

4 thickly-cut sirloin steaks

1 tablesp butter

a few dashes of olive oil

60 ml/2 fl oz Irish whiskey

300 ml/10 fl oz double cream

sea salt and freshly ground black pepper

Method:

Heat a large heavy-based pan and when it is smoking hot add the oil and butter and then, after a few seconds, the steaks. Cook for 4–5 minutes on each side (the exact time depends on the thickness of the steaks and how you like your meat cooked). Rest the steaks in a warm place while you make the sauce.

Discard excess fat from the pan. Deglaze the pan with the whiskey, allowing it to bubble up but not dry out completely. Add the cream and simmer until the sauce thickens. Season to taste with black pepper and salt. Serve the steaks surrounded by the sauce. Garnish with sliced mushrooms cooked in a small knob of butter until their juices are reabsorbed.

BEEF SAUSAGES WITH ONION GRAVY AND CHAMP

Traditionally, fresh sausages are made from pork but nowadays creative craft butchers make speciality sausages using lamb and even furred and feathered game. In Northern Ireland you'll see beef sausages on offer in every butcher's window and on menus from workplace canteens to cafés, pubs and even fine-dining establishments. The traditional accompaniment, which again is much more a part of the daily diet in Northern Ireland, is champ, usually with the added frill of a spoonful of onion gravy.

SERVES 4

Ingredients:

4–8 (depending on size) meaty beef sausages

90 g/3 oz butter

450 g/1 lb onions, peeled and finely chopped

1 tablesp plain white flour

300 ml/10 fl oz well-flavoured beef stock

For the champ:

900 g/2lbs floury potatoes

1 large bunch scallions (about 1 cup), chopped

250 ml/8 fl oz/ 1 cup milk

butter to taste

Method:

Melt the butter in a heavy-based pan. Add the onions and cook them over a gentle heat very slowly until well browned. Sprinkle on the flour, stirring until it begins to brown. Gradually add the stock, stirring to prevent lumps forming. Simmer for a further 15 minutes to allow the flavour to develop.

Cook the sausages. In Northern Ireland they would be fried slowly, but as long as you keep the heat low, they may be grilled, or set on a rack and cooked in the oven. Large meaty sausages should always be cooked slowly and turned frequently so that they brown evenly on all sides.

To make Champ:

Steam the potatoes (preferably in their skins). Dry using an absorbent cloth or tea towel, then peel. Chop the scallions and simmer in the milk for a minute or two. Put the potatoes through a potato ricer or mouli, or mash thoroughly. Add the milk and scallion mixture, season to taste and mix thoroughly. You may add more milk if the mixture seems dry, but on no account should it become wet.

Reheat until piping hot. This can be done most conveniently in a microwave oven at a medium setting for 5–7 minutes. Place each serving on a very hot plate, make a 'dunt' (depression) in the centre and put a good knob of butter in, allowing it to melt into a little lake. Eat from the outside in, dipping each forkful in the butter.

Serve the sausages with a little gravy poured over them and the champ on the side.

STEAK AND KIDNEY PUDDING

A dish that takes a little time. You must begin the preparations the evening before you want to cook and eat it. Irish ale is quite different from English beer; it has a distinctive, slightly bitter, taste of hops.

SERVES 4

Ingredients:

- 700 g/1½ lb shin of beef
- 300 ml/10 fl oz ale
- 2 tablesp oil
- ½ tablesp fresh tarragon leaves, chopped
- one onion, peeled and chopped
- 350 g/12 oz ox (beef) kidney
- 1 tablesp Irish mustard
- 300 ml/10 fl oz milk
- 300 ml/10 fl oz beef stock

For the pudding crust:

- 560 g/1¼ lb white flour
- 110 g/4 oz beef suet, finely chopped, or grated
- 1 egg yolk
- 90 ml/3 fl oz milk
- 1 teasp black treacle
- salt and pepper

Method:

Clean and remove any membrane and fat from the kidney; cut into thin, bite-sized slices and soak in milk overnight in the fridge. Remove any excess fat or very large pieces of gristle from the beef and cut into bite-sized cubes; place in a bowl with the ale, oil and tarragon and marinate overnight in the fridge.

Next day, fry the onion in a little oil until golden brown. Use a slotted spoon to remove meat cubes from the marinade and roll them in seasoned flour. Add the beef cubes to the onion pan a few at a time and brown lightly on all sides. Add the marinade, mustard and the stock; bring to simmering point and cook gently for one hour. Strain the milk from the kidney; add the kidney to the stew and simmer for another 45 minutes. The meat will become tender and the gravy rich (if it seems a bit on the pale side add a dash of gravy browning).

While cooking the steak and kidney, make

the suet crust. Sift flour into a bowl and stir in the suet. Mix egg yolk, treacle and milk and add this to the mixture. Mix well and knead briefly and lightly. Cover with cling-film and rest in the fridge for 30 minutes. Take about three-quarters of the dough and roll it out to line a 1½ litre/ 2½ lb pudding bowl. Roll out the remaining dough to make a lid for the top.

Line the bowl. Pour in the meat and gravy. Place the lid on top and pinch the edges securely together. Take a large piece of double-thickness foil, grease it with a little oil and wrap up the pudding bowl well. Place on a rack in a steamer and steam steadily, covered, for one and a half hours. Check the water level regularly, adding more if necessary. This pudding is traditionally eaten with carrots and steamed potatoes.

BEEF AND OYSTER PIES

An interesting combination of three foods much loved in Ireland: beef, stout and oysters. The reason why this must be cooked in a two-stage process is that oysters need only light cooking and become tough if overcooked.

SERVES 4

Ingredients:

900 g/2 lb stewing beef, well trimmed of fat, and cut into bite-sized pieces

2 onions, peeled and sliced

2 tablesp rendered beef fat, or oil

300 ml/10 fl oz stout

1 tablesp flour

salt and freshly ground black pepper

2 bay leaves

1 sprig thyme

2 tablesp parsley, chopped

350 g/12 oz puff pastry

a dozen oysters, opened, removed from the shell and their juices saved

Method:

Heat half the beef fat or oil in a large pan. Add the onions and cook gently until soft and beginning to brown; remove from the pan and set aside. Add the remaining fat or oil. Raise the heat and add the beef, a few pieces at a time. Brown lightly on all sides. Sprinkle over the flour and stir until browned. Return onions to the pan. Pour in the stout, stirring to release any crispy bits from the pan. Season with salt and pepper. Add bay leaves, thyme and parsley. Cover and simmer very gently for about 1½–2 hours, or until the meat is tender (time will depend on the cut/quality of the meat). Alternatively, braise in an oven at 160°C/325°F/Gas 3. Cool fully. Divide the shelled oysters and their juice between four individual pie dishes. Gently mix into the meat mix. Roll out the pastry larger than the pie dish. Dampen the rim of the dish and press the pastry down with a fork or pastry crimper. Cut a small hole in the top of each pie to let steam escape. Brush with a little milk. Bake at 200°C/400°F/Gas 6 for 15 minutes. Lower heat to 180°C/350°F/Gas 4 and bake for a further 20–25 minutes, or until the meat is hot through. The traditional accompaniment is a glass of stout.

BEEF FILLET BAKED IN A TURF CRUST

This comes from Evan Doyle in The Strawberry Tree restaurant at the Brooklodge Hotel, Macreddin Village, near Aughrim, County Wicklow. Evan writes of this unusual recipe: 'This is a recipe that we have the opportunity to use both for large functions like weddings and also for smaller numbers in the restaurant. It's a very, very simple recipe that's based on salt crust baking, but uses peat moss [milled turf] instead and to the same end effect — the moisture of the meat being trapped inside by the turf produces a really moist and juicy dish on the inside, enhanced by an earthy, Irishy "terroir" flavour on the outside. For a small amount of beef, as in a fillet for 2 or 4 people, a 1 kg/2lb loaf tin can be used; for larger cuts like half a strip sirloin, a large deep baking dish is perfect. As in salt crusting, line the base with an inch of turf, place the meat on top and then completely cover with more turf and press firm. Sprinkle with a small amount of water and cover with fork-pricked tin foil.'

The following recipe is for a large party.

Method:

Ingredients:

1 striploin, or fillet, of organic beef

1 bag of peat moss

salt, black pepper

Season the beef very well with the salt and pepper, rubbing in all over. Line the base of a deep baking dish with a layer of peat moss, place the meat into the tin and cover completely with more peat, pressing it until it is firm. Put into a pre-heated oven at 160°C/325°F/Gas 3 and cook for 1½ to 2 hours depending on size. Because you cannot make visual checks or test with a skewer, it's essential to use a meat probe to test the internal temperature of the meat at the centre of the joint. A temperature of 50°C will give you rare meat. Break the crust, lift out the meat and use kitchen paper to remove the attached turf, leaving just a fine, fine covering for taste. Let it rest for 15–20 minutes, then slice and serve.

BEEF AND STOUT STEW

In Ireland beef stews often contain stout or beer instead of, or as well as, stock or water. Like all Irish stews it is eaten with mounds of floury potatoes, but it is also quite common for the potatoes to be cooked in the pot with the stew (added towards the end of cooking time). In Dublin the preferred cut of meat would be shin beef because when given long, slow cooking it softens to a melting tenderness and produces thick, rich, gelatinous gravy.

SERVES 4

Ingredients:

450–700 g/1 lb–1½ lb shin beef

2 large onions, peeled and chopped

2–3 carrots, peeled and sliced

30 g/1 oz/2 tablesp butter or beef dripping

pot herbs (bay, parsley, thyme)

225 ml/8 fl oz/1 cup stout or beer

225 ml/8 fl oz/1 cup water

salt and freshly ground black pepper

Method:

Melt the fat in a large frying pan and fry the onions gently until translucent and beginning to brown at the edges. Remove them with a slotted spoon and place with the carrots in the bottom of a casserole. Remove the outer membrane from the beef and any large sinews and gristle. Cut the meat into rounds about 2 cm/1 inch thick and brown quickly in the hot fat to seal them. Remove the meat from the pan and put in the casserole on top of the vegetables. Deglaze the frying pan with the stout or beer. Add this liquid to the casserole along with the water, pot herbs and seasoning. Cover tightly and cook slowly in a pre-heated oven at 160°C/325°F/Gas 3 for 3 hours.

You may need to thicken the gravy with flour if you use a cut other than shin beef; do this by dusting the meat pieces in seasoned flour before sealing them in the pan. It can be further enriched by adding ox or lamb's kidney. The stew improves in flavour if refrigerated and reheated after a day or two.

POTTED BEEF

This recipe is delicious, keeps well, freezes well, and makes you wonder why people do not buy cheap cuts of meat any more. The inclusion of a pig's trotter helps it set better.

SERVES 8–10

Ingredients:

1 kg/2 lb boneless shin beef

1 marrowbone, sawn in half

1 pig's trotter (optional)

2 large carrots, peeled

1 bay leaf

1 large onion, peeled and studded with 6–8 cloves

½ teasp ground mace

a pinch of cayenne pepper

a pinch of ground ginger

salt and freshly ground black pepper

Method:

Put the meat, marrowbone and trotter (if using) into a stockpot with the carrots, onions and bay leaf. Cover with cold water and bring to a gentle simmer, skimming off any scum that rises. Simmer for 3–4 hours until the meat is completely tender. Remove the meat from the water and refrigerate. Remove the bone and vegetables and cool the stock in the fridge (ideally overnight), then remove any set fat from the surface.

Warm the stock again and strain it thoroughly. Boil it hard until it has reduced by half. It should taste beefy but not too rich. Pass the cold beef and some of the meat and skin from the pig's trotter through a coarse mincer. Transfer to a mixing bowl and moisten with up to two ladles of the stock (you want to keep it soft and spreadable). Season with the spices and the salt and pepper, tasting as you go; mix well. Pile into a terrine dish (don't press it down too much) and ladle over just enough stock to cover the meat. Place it to set in the fridge. Good with bread and salad leaves, or as a filling for rolls and sandwiches.

LAMB

In Ireland sheep were kept primarily for their wool and they were milked. There are very few references to eating sheep meat in ancient times and it was probably eaten only when a beast died through misadventure or old age. That modern favourite, prime tender young lamb, was certainly a rarity; nor would seared lamb steaks and the like feature in traditional Irish cooking. Instead you find slow-cooked dishes with lots of vegetables (and often grains) to bulk out relatively small quantities of meat.

Irish Stew is probably our best-known dish beyond these shores. Properly prepared, Irish stew will make a good meal of the most ancient ewe. There is a tradition that claims that the original meat for Irish stew was goat meat. This would make sense because there were always domesticated goats in Ireland (we still have wild goats), and bones from goats have been found at the earliest cooking sites and habitations.

E. Estyn Evans claimed that the goat, along with the donkey, became a symbol of poverty in post-famine Ireland and was so despised that the keeping of goats and the making of goat's milk cheese died out. Yet the goat is an ideal animal to graze much of our rough hill pasture. It has made a comeback. Artisan food producers have developed excellent goat's cheese, milk and yoghurt. While an old goat is still pretty unpalatable and better treated, as one book has it, 'like bad venison', tender kid is a delicate meat and now available once more.

I have had a delicious Irish stew made from kid, but Irish stew is made today from mutton or lamb. Mutton is essential, according to the purists. I've never been dogmatic and, like most people, prefer lamb, or at least a beast that has not celebrated its first birthday. Modern Irish chefs have transformed this simple white stew into an often complicated and refined dish but the basic recipe is not to be despised; its very simplicity makes it so enduring.

IRISH STEW

SERVES 4

Ingredients:

1.4 kg/3 lb potatoes, peeled

900 g/2 lb stewing lamb
(gigot or neck)

450 g/1 lb onions, chopped

5 tablesp fresh parsley,
chopped

1 tablesp fresh thyme,
chopped

250–500 ml/8–16 fl oz/1–2
cups of water

salt and freshly ground black
pepper

Method:

Peel the potatoes. Leave them whole unless very large. The bones in the meat and a certain amount of fat are essential to the flavour of Irish stew as the potatoes absorb a good deal of the fat and flavour of the meat. The meat is not cubed but left in fairly large pieces. When the meat is cooked enough it falls away from the bone, which then poses no hazard on the plate.

Place a layer of onion on the bottom of a heavy pot or casserole. Lay the meat on this. Season with the salt and pepper and sprinkle generously with fresh parsley and much less generously with chopped thyme. Layer the rest of the onions with the potatoes and finish with the rest of the herbs. The amount of water you add depends on how good the seal is between pot and lid. Bring to the boil and cover tightly. You may either simmer gently on the hob or cook in the oven at 150°C/300°F/Gas2 for 2½–3 hours.

The finished stew should be moist but definitely not 'swimming' in liquid. Add a little hot water during cooking only if it appears to be getting too dry for your taste. Floury potatoes will partly dissolve into the liquid, thickening it a little; waxy potatoes will not. It's a matter of taste which you use – I use some of both.

Serve with lots of chopped parsley. Carrots, which should be cooked separately and never in the stew, are the perfect accompaniment.

Lamb, Carrot and Barley Casserole

This traditional dish was designed to make a little lamb go a long way, especially if served with tender spring cabbage and baked floury potatoes. It balances a large amount of carrots with the same amount of meat, and the barley swells to add more strength to a dense stew.

SERVES 4–5

Ingredients:

700 g/1½ lb stewing lamb (gigot, neck, or boned and well-trimmed breast)

1 tablesp butter or lamb fat

2 onions, peeled and chopped

700 g/1½ lb carrots, thickly sliced

4 sticks celery, chopped

3 tablesp pearl barley

lamb or vegetable stock (enough to cover)

a few sprigs of thyme or marjoram

a handful of parsley, chopped

salt and freshly ground black pepper

Method:

Cut the lamb into bite-sized pieces and brown in butter or a little rendered lamb fat in a flame-proof casserole. Add all the chopped vegetables and fry them for a minute or two. Rinse the barley under running water, drain and add to the casserole. Season with freshly ground black pepper and a little salt. Add just enough stock to cover the meat and vegetables. Cover tightly and simmer gently on the hob or cook in the oven at 150°C/300°F/Gas 2 for one and a half hours, or until the lamb is really tender. If it looks like drying out, add a little extra stock or water. Just before serving sprinkle the top generously with the parsley.

LAMB STEAKS WITH FRESH, SPICED TOMATO CHUTNEY

Take care not to overcook these steaks; Irish lamb is at its very best when served pink and juicy.

SERVES 4

Ingredients:

4 lamb steaks

1 tablesp olive oil

1 tablesp balsamic vinegar

freshly ground black pepper

For the tomato chutney:

1 x 450 g/1 lb can of plum tomatoes

1 teasp sugar

1 tablesp cider vinegar

1 teasp cardamom pods

½ teasp cumin seeds

2 bay leaves

1-inch piece of fresh ginger, peeled and finely chopped

freshly ground black pepper and salt to taste

Method:

Prepare the chutney. De-seed the cardamom pods, discarding the woody outer kernel. Chop the tomatoes and place with all the other ingredients (except the salt and pepper) in a pot. Bring to the boil, reduce heat and simmer until the mixture becomes thick and pulpy. Season to taste with salt and black pepper. Cool to room temperature.

Rub the lamb steaks on both sides with the oil and balsamic vinegar; season with black pepper. Grill or cook on a barbecue for 2–4 minutes on each side (the exact time depends on the thickness of the steaks and how you like your lamb cooked). Season with a sprinkle of sea salt and serve with a mixed green leaf salad and the chutney.

BRAISED RUMP OF LAMB

This slow-cooked method for cooking lamb is full of flavour and an ideal way of preparing less tender cuts of lamb.

SERVES 4

Ingredients:

4 pieces of rump of lamb (or other suitable cut for braising)

1 tablesp olive oil

a small sprig of rosemary

1–2 cloves garlic, peeled

3 large carrots, peeled and chopped

2 medium onions, peeled and chopped

1 large (or two small) leeks, cleaned and chopped

90 g/3 oz fresh parsley, including stalks

450 g/1 lb ripe tomatoes, chopped

¼ teasp sugar

2 tablesp tomato purée

150 ml/5 fl oz red wine

75 ml/2½ fl oz port

375 ml/12 fl oz meat stock (lamb, beef, or chicken)

4 bay leaves

salt and black pepper

Method:

First brown the meat on all sides in oil over a high heat. Add the garlic and rosemary when nearly browned to flavour the oil. Place meat in a deep roasting tin. Add carrots, onions and leeks to the pan and fry for a minute or two. Add tomatoes, sugar, parsley and tomato purée and bring to the boil. Add red wine, port and stock. Cook fairly fast for about five minutes to reduce the amount of liquid. Pour over the meat in the roasting tin. Add bay leaves. Cover tightly with foil and cook at 150°C/300°F/Gas 2 for about three-quarters of an hour, or until the lamb is tender. Take up lamb and keep warm while you finish the sauce. Strain the liquid from the roasting tin into a wide pan. Cook fast to reduce the liquid. It should be thick enough to describe the resulting sauce as a glaze. Serve at once poured over the lamb.

LAMB HEARTS IN RED WINE WITH APRICOT AND HAZELNUT STUFFING

Hazelnuts still grow wild in many parts of Ireland and have been an important food since man arrived here. They have an affinity with lamb and add texture and flavour to a stuffing. This is a dish best made with young spring lamb hearts.

SERVES 4

Ingredients:

4 spring lamb hearts

1 level tablesp paprika and 1 of flour, mixed

1 tablesp olive oil

150 ml/5 fl oz red wine

125–150 ml/4–5 fl oz water

For the stuffing:

1 small onion, finely chopped

1 tablesp butter

4–6 dried apricots, very finely chopped

60 g/2 oz hazelnuts, very finely chopped

60 g/2 oz fresh breadcrumbs

4 tablesp parsley, finely chopped

2 teasp fresh thyme, finely chopped

salt and freshly ground black pepper

Method:

First make the stuffing. Melt butter in a small pan. Add the chopped onion and cook over a gentle heat until soft but not browned; add the rest of the stuffing ingredients and mix well.

Prepare the lamb hearts by washing, de-fatting, cutting out any tubes that have not been removed by the butcher, and drying on kitchen paper. Press the stuffing firmly into the cavity of each lamb heart. Secure the opening with cocktail sticks or small skewers. Roll to coat with the paprika and flour mixture. Choose a small flame- and oven-proof pot just big enough to fit the hearts snugly. Heat the olive oil in the pan; seal and brown the hearts on all sides. Pour over the wine and bubble briefly over a high heat. Add 125 ml/4 fl oz of the water. Cover with a tight-fitting lid to prevent the liquid from evaporating. Place in a preheated oven at 160°C/325°F/Gas 3. Cook until they are very tender when tested with a thin skewer; depending on the age of the lamb this will take about 1½–2 hours. If too much liquid evaporates add a little extra water.

Serve with champ [see recipe page 17/18] or colcannon, and buttered carrots or parsnips.

RACK OF LAMB WITH A HERB CRUST AND PEA AND MINT CHAMP

A dinner party dish for 4–6 people. Racks contain 7 (tiny) chops and while some people are content with two chops, meat lovers might consider three a mean serving!

Ingredients:

2 racks of spring lamb, trimmed and chined by the butcher

For the herb crust:

30 g/1 oz butter, melted

2 tablesp mild Irish mustard

4 tablesp olive oil

150 g/5 oz fine white breadcrumbs

2 sprigs each of rosemary, mint and parsley, finely chopped

1–2 cloves garlic, peeled, crushed and finely chopped

zest of one lemon

For the pea and mint champ:

450 g/1 lb floury potatoes cooked, peeled and mashed while hot

450 g/1 lb peas, cooked

150 ml/5 fl oz cream

30 g/1 oz butter

2–3 tablesp fresh mint, chopped

salt and freshly ground black pepper

Method:

Trim excess fat from the lamb, leaving just a thin layer. Wrap the ends of the bones with foil to prevent burning. Seal the fatty side of the racks quickly in a hot pan in a little oil. Take up and cool. Mix the butter with the mustard and spread this on the fatty side of each rack. Mix the rest of the herb crust mixture together and divide between the two racks, spreading over the fatty side and pressing it down firmly. Roast at 180°C/350°F/Gas 4 for about 25 minutes for pink juicy meat. Rest before carving into cutlets.

Whiz peas and mint in a food processor or blender until smooth. Heat the cream and butter and stir in the peas and the mashed potatoes; beat thoroughly so that everything is well mixed. Season to taste with salt and black pepper and stir over a low heat until everything is hot through.

ROAST STUFFED LAMB WITH RHUBARB

A simple family roast that combines favourite flavours and is quick and easy to prepare.

SERVES 6

Ingredients:

1 kg/2¼ lb boned loin of lamb

one small onion, peeled and finely chopped

30 g/1 oz butter

2–3 (depending on size) sticks of young rhubarb, finely diced

30 g/1 oz fine breadcrumbs

2 tablesp fresh mint, finely chopped

2 tablesp medium sherry

125 ml/4 fl oz lamb stock

Method:

Remove outer skin and excess fat from the lamb and lay out flat. Season with half the mint, the salt and freshly ground black pepper.

Melt the butter in a small pan and fry the onion with the remaining mint until soft but not coloured; add two thirds of the rhubarb and cook for a few seconds. Take off the heat, stir in the breadcrumbs and season with a little more salt and freshly ground black pepper. Place stuffing in the centre of the loin, roll up and tie securely with string in several places along its length. Seal in a little oil in a very hot pan and then transfer to a preheated oven at 180°C/350°F/Gas 4 for about 30 minutes per kg (15 minutes per lb).

Take up the lamb and allow to rest while you finish the sauce. Pour off excess fat from the cooking pan. Add the remaining rhubarb to the pan, deglaze with sherry, then add the lamb stock. Bubble up until the rhubarb juice runs and the sauce reaches a slightly syrupy consistency. Strain and serve with slices of lamb garnished with some fresh sprigs of mint.

Lamb's Liver with Dry-cured Bacon

Lamb's liver is by far the most popular liver eaten in Ireland; calf liver is only occasionally available and pork liver, while still used for pâtés and terrines, is not now eaten 'neat' except by older people.

SERVES 4

Ingredients:

400 g/14 oz lamb's liver, thinly sliced

1–2 tablesp butter

1–2 teasp oil

8 rashers (slices) of dry-cured bacon

2 large tomatoes, halved

1–2 tablesp flour, seasoned with salt and a little pepper

Method:

If the slices of liver are thick use a very sharp knife to slice them more thinly lengthways. Lay out a plate of seasoned flour and preheat a large pan. Meanwhile grill or pan-fry the bacon until the fat is crisp and cook the tomatoes, seasoned with salt and black pepper, with the bacon until soft.

Dust the liver in the seasoned flour. Melt the butter and oil in the pan and quickly fry the liver, turning just once. Thin slices take just one to two minutes on each side; watch the time carefully because liver can quickly become tough and leathery. Dish up at once with the bacon and tomatoes.

Good served with white or wholemeal soda bread and butter.

TRADITIONAL DINGLE PIES

As any visitor to Kerry will know, there are a lot of sheep on the Dingle peninsula and they live a good life, roaming the hills and grazing on land rich in natural herbiage that gives the meat a particularly good flavour. Dingle is a food-lover's destination, with many good restaurants and pubs which serve fine food. This recipe comes from John Benny Moriarty who serves Dingle pies in his pub, John Benny's, on Strand Street, Dingle.

MAKES 4 PIES

Ingredients:
For the filling:

700 g/1 ½ lb mutton or mature lamb (a cut with a good proportion of bone and fat is needed, eg gigot or shoulder; the aim is to end up with about 350 g /12 oz very lean meat for the pies, with the remaining fatty meat and bones for the stock)

a little chopped parsley and fresh thyme

1 onion, chopped

For the stock:

1 carrot, chopped

1 stick celery, chopped

1 leek, chopped

a handful of parsley

a good-sized branch of thyme

a few bay leaves

salt and pepper

water to cover

For the pastry:

250 g/ 8 oz plain white flour

60 g/ 2 oz rendered lamb fat and/or other hard fat such as lard, beef dripping, butter or hard margarine

about 150 ml/ 5 fl oz water

½ teasp salt

Method:

Prepare the meat by trimming off all fat, fatty meat and bones. Cut the lean meat into small pieces and set aside while you make the stock. Place the bones and trimmings in a stock pot, add the vegetables and herbs, salt and pepper. Cover with water, bring to the boil and skim off any scum. Simmer for a few hours. Strain and place in a large jug in the fridge. When the fat solidifies use a slotted spoon to lift it off carefully. Weigh the fat and if it is less than 60 g/ 2 oz, make up the difference with one of the hard fats suggested in the ingredients list.

Make the pastry by rubbing the fat into the flour and salt, adding enough water to make a soft dough. Knead, rest for a while, then roll out fairly thickly. Cut into 8 rounds the size of a saucer, about 12–13 cm (5 inches) in diameter. Traditionally, the lid of a metal saucepan with a sharp rim is used to cut the shape.

Divide the meat between 4 of the pastry rounds. Place it in a mound in the centre of the pastry. Moisten with a little of the stock. Add the chopped parsley and thyme and season well with salt and pepper. Place a second round of pastry on top. Dampen the edges and fix them firmly together with a round-bladed knife. Cut a hole in the top to allow steam to escape. Bake on a non-stick baking tray in an oven preheated to 180°C/350°F/Gas 4 for about 45 minutes, or until nicely browned on top.

The pies are served hot in a large soup bowl with the boiling stock poured over them, but can also be kept until needed in a cool place and reheated gently in a low oven before serving with the stock.

Pork

The pig was the favourite food of the native Irish. The earliest sagas, the ancient laws, the rules of monasteries, even the granting of rights of pannage (grazing rights of the woods) by the Normans to their tenants attest to the importance of the pig in Irish food culture. While cattle, sheep and goats may be kept for other products like milk, butter, hides and wool, the pig provides only meat and it was for meat it was kept.

Once known as the 'gentleman who paid the rent', pigs used to be as numerous in Ireland as people. Pigs were killed and cured at the home place and everything but the squeal was used – we have more recipes for the various parts of the pig than for any other animal. While some pork was eaten fresh, much of it was salted and cured to make it last the winter (or the year), because a household might have only a single pig to last the year. Despite this, when they killed their pig, they would still send choice morsels of fresh pork – the liver, pork fillet steak, fresh sausage, puddings and brawn (potted head cheese) to neighbours and expect to get the same in return when a neighbour killed a pig. It was a tradition that went back a long way.

Stephen Gwynn described the divisions of the pig that were common in 1600: 'The head, tongue and feet to the smith, the neck to the butcher, the 2 small ribs that go with the hindquarters to the tailor, the kidneys to the physician, the udder to the harper, the liver to the carpenter and the sweetbreads to her that is with child'.

Today, production is by a combination of large-scale manufacturers (for both home and export markets), artisan producers and many craft butchers specialising in pork, both fresh and cured.

Pork, fresh and cured, is eaten at every meal of the day. Fresh pork is usually simply cooked: grilled pork chops, pork roasts and pork stews are the principal methods. Kidneys are a beloved delicacy, eaten grilled, often with a spicy devilled sauce. While some people like fried pig's liver, it is more usually made into pâté.

ROAST LOIN OF FARMED BOAR STUFFED WITH POITÍN-SOAKED PRUNES

WITH BLACK PUDDING MASH AND VANILLA FROTH

Wild boar no longer exist in Ireland. But farmed 'wild boar' is bred, reared and allowed to range freely on the Moyallon Estate in Northern Ireland. This recipe was devised by Derry Clarke of L'Écrivain restaurant in Dublin to celebrate the excellence of this award-winning product. You can also make the dish with fresh pork fillet or loin instead of boar.

SERVES 4

Ingredients:

700 g/1 ½ lb boned loin of 'wild boar'

125 ml/4 fl oz Irish poitín (or white wine)

8 prunes, stoned

salt and freshly ground black pepper

For the vanilla froth:

2 shallots, peeled and finely chopped

a knob of butter

½ a vanilla pod, seeds removed

1 tablesp white wine

90 ml/3 fl oz chicken stock

150 ml/5 fl oz cream

For the black pudding mash:

a knob of butter

225 g/8 oz black pudding, skinned and broken up

60 g/2 oz smoked bacon, finely chopped

30 g/1 oz shallots, peeled and finely chopped

90 ml/3 fl oz cream

225 g/8 oz cooked potatoes, mashed while hot

Method:

Soak the prunes overnight in poitín or wine. Use a skewer to make a circular probe-shaped incision through the middle length of the loin and stuff the prunes into it. Now place a square of foil on a flat surface. On top place a square of cling-film. Place the loin at one end and roll up tightly. Chill for two hours. Remove foil and cling-film and cut the meat into four steaks with a sharp knife. Sear on a hot pan on both sides to brown. Transfer to a roasting tin and finish the cooking in an oven set to 200°C/400°F/Gas 6 for 7–10 minutes. Allow to rest a while before serving.

Make the black pudding mash by melting the butter in a heavy saucepan and cooking the shallot and bacon until soft. Add the black pudding. Stir over a moderate heat for 2 minutes. Add the cream and potatoes and heat through; keep warm until you are ready to serve.

Make the vanilla froth by frying the finely chopped shallot in the butter until softened; add the vanilla, wine and chicken stock. Cook until a syrupy consistency is reached. Add the cream and heat gently until warm. Remove the vanilla pod. Using a whisk or hand blender, whisk up to a froth. Place the loin of boar with the black pudding mash on hot serving plates and surround with the vanilla froth.

spiceδ slow-roasteδ belly of pork

with apple, thyme anδ cream sauce

This dish has become so popular with food writers as a posh but inexpensive dinner party dish that it's easy to forget that it was created by Gerry Galvin, one of the earliest and most influential pioneers of the new Irish cuisine. It has a very traditional herb stuffing but the usual accompaniment of apple sauce is transformed into a subtle and rich one. The spicy paste might seem un-Irish but the ingredients are traditional and, apart from the lemon, are all grown and made in Ireland.

SERVES 6–8

Ingredients:

1.4 kg/3 lb pork belly, boned, skinned and trimmed of excess fat

For the stuffing:

1 medium onion, finely chopped

2–3 cloves garlic, peeled, crushed and chopped

90 g/3 oz butter

4–5 tablesp mixed fresh herbs (parsley, thyme, marjoram and a leaf of sage)

225 g/8 oz fresh breadcrumbs

1 egg, beaten

For the spiced paste:

2 tablesp butter, melted

2 tablesp fruit chutney

salt and black pepper

1 tablesp lemon juice

2 cloves garlic, peeled, crushed and chopped

1 tablesp fresh thyme, chopped

2 tablesp Irish mustard

For the apple sauce:

2 medium-sized cooking apples (preferably Bramley), cored, peeled and roughly chopped

1 medium onion, peeled and roughly chopped

2 cloves garlic, peeled and crushed

2 sprigs thyme

125 ml/4 fl oz medium-sweet white wine

125 ml/4 fl oz chicken stock

250 ml/8 fl oz cream

Method:

First make the herb stuffing by melting the butter in a small pan and cooking the onion and garlic in it until soft. Take off the heat and stir in the herbs and breadcrumbs. When cooled a little, add the egg and season with salt and pepper.

Use a fork to prick the inner side of the meat. Combine the spiced paste ingredients. Brush half the paste over the inside of the meat, then spread the stuffing over this. Roll up the joint and tie firmly with cotton string. Set oven to 150°C/300°F/Gas 2 and while it's heating brown the meat in a little oil. Place the meat seam side up on a rack in a roasting tin and roast for 3 hours in all. About half way through the roasting time, brush the meat on all sides with the remaining paste and then replace, seam side down, on the rack.

Make the apple sauce by placing all the ingredients in a pot and simmering them for about 15 minutes. Take out the thyme and then whiz the sauce in a food processor or blender. Strain. If it appears too thick you may add a little extra stock. Serve hot with the meat cut into reasonably thick slices.

pork steak with mustard sauce and apple champ

The pork steak, or fillet as it is more usually called, has been a treasured cut of the pig for centuries. It is quickly cooked; its natural tenderness is spoiled by overcooking.

SERVES 4–6

Ingredients:

2 pork fillets

2 tablesp butter

2 teasp olive oil

60 ml/2 fl oz dry cider or white wine

200 ml/7 fl oz cream

4 tablesp mild mustard (a mild, course-grained Irish, or Dijon)

For the apple champ:

900 g/ 2 lbs floury potatoes, peeled

450g/1 lb cooking apples (Bramleys or similar fluffy apple)

1 teasp chopped fresh sage (optional)

salt and freshly ground black pepper

Method:

Heat two non-stick pans until hot but not smoking. Add equal amounts of butter to each and as soon as it sizzles add one fillet to each pan. Cook, turning once, until browned on each side and cooked through but still juicy. This will take 6–8 minutes. Take them up and leave to rest in a warm place.

Use half the cider to deglaze one pan and pour the resulting juices into the second pan together with the rest of the cider and deglaze the second pan quickly. Add cream and mustard and whisk everything together. Cook over a moderate heat until the sauce thickens and reaches a pleasing consistency.

For the champ, steam the potatoes until tender, then put through a potato ricer or mouli, or mash until lump-free. Slice the apples and cook until soft in just 2 tablesp of water. Beat with a wooden spoon until completely smooth. Mix into the potato with the sage, salt and black pepper. Slice the pork before serving.

Poultry

The rearing of poultry was woman's work and for centuries the money earned allowed rural Irish women to buy luxuries they might not have been able to afford otherwise. Small wonder they took it seriously and reared geese, ducks, hens, sometimes guinea fowl, pigeons and, after their introduction in the seventeenth century, turkeys. A more recent addition to farmed poultry is quail. Although an indigenous wild bird, most today are farmed by artisan food producers; they are sold in some supermarkets and specialist shops but mainly appear on the menus of upmarket restaurants. Chicken is produced commercially in vast quantities for home and export markets and is the everyday bird – unless you buy a truly free-range, organic bird, which always deserves special treatment.

MICHAELMAS ROAST GOOSE

For centuries, from September to Christmas, this was the bird served at weddings and for Sunday dinner in well-to-do households. The goose once vied with roast beef as the main dish on Christmas Day. From Norman times, Michaelmas (29 September, the feast day of St Michael the Archangel) was a hiring or rent day in parts of the country – in Carlow in 1305 a goose was worth twenty pennies and a landlord would accept the money or a goose as his rent. In later times the feast became one of the days of the year on which farmers killed an animal and gave food to their poorer neighbours. It was, very often, a goose (or two) from the flocks kept by their wives! In the apple-growing areas of Ireland – Munster and south Ulster – this was the day on which the apple harvest began, a time to make cider to serve with a goose and baked apples.

SERVES 6–8

Ingredients:

1 goose (about 4.5 kg/10 lb) with giblets

potato stuffing (see recipe on page 46)

1 onion, sliced

2 carrots, sliced

2 celery sticks, sliced

a small bunch of parsley and thyme

75 ml/2½ fl oz dry cider

1 tablesp plain flour

chopped watercress or parsley to garnish

Method:

Put the giblets in a pan with the onion, carrots, celery and herbs. Cover with cold water. (I always remove the liver to fry in butter, flame in whiskey and then eat as a delight with hot buttered toast.) Season, then simmer for 35–40 minutes to make a stock for the gravy. Strain the stock.

Preheat oven to 200°C/400°F/Gas 6.

Wipe out the goose and stuff the neck cavity with the potato stuffing from the next recipe. Weigh the stuffed goose and calculate the cooking time at 15 minutes per 450 g/1 lb and 15 minutes over. Always allow at least another 20 minutes resting time when calculating the time at which you will serve the goose. Prick the skin all over with a fork, sprinkle generously with salt and pepper and rub these in well. Put the goose on a rack in a large roasting pan, cover with foil and put it into the preheated oven.

After an hour, remove the goose from the oven and pour off the fat that has accumulated in the roasting pan (strain this and reserve in a jar in the fridge for roasting potatoes; it keeps for months). Pour the dry cider over the goose and return to the oven. Half an hour before the end of the estimated cooking time remove the foil and baste the bird with the juices. Return to the oven, uncovered, and allow the bird to brown and the skin to crisp. When cooked, transfer to a heated serving dish and put it in a warm place to rest for about twenty minutes.

Make the gravy by pouring off any excess fat from the roasting pan, leaving only about two tablespoons. Sprinkle in enough plain flour to absorb this and cook over a medium heat for a minute or so, scraping up the sediments on the bottom of the pan. Stir in enough giblet stock to make a gravy, bring it to the boil and, stirring constantly, simmer for a few minutes (add any juices that have accumulated under the resting bird), season to taste and pour the gravy into a heated sauceboat.

Remove the potato stuffing from the goose into a heated bowl. Carve the goose into slices, mixing breast and leg. Serve goose and stuffing garnished with chopped watercress (or parsley) and the gravy.

POTATO STUFFING

In Kerry this stuffing is known as 'pandy'. No goose is complete without a generous amount of potato stuffing to soak up some of the gorgeous fat. The herb you choose is up to you. If the stuffing is for pork, goose or duck, fresh sage is traditional, thyme, winter savoury and parsley are other possibilities, either singly or mixed.

Ingredients:

900 g/2 lbs floury potatoes, cooked, dried and mashed

450 g/1 lb onion, peeled and chopped

2 large apples, peeled, cored and chopped (optional)

225 g/½ lb lean sausage meat (optional)

1 tablesp butter, or goose fat, or duck fat

2 tablesp fresh herbs, finely chopped

salt and freshly ground black pepper

Method:

Put the potatoes in a large mixing bowl. Melt the butter or goose fat in a pan and in it sweat the chopped onion and apple. Pan-fry the sausage meat, breaking it up with a fork until browned and cooked through. Add the onion, apple, cooked sausage meat (if using) and herbs to the potatoes. Season to taste with salt (very little if you are using sausage meat) and freshly ground black pepper. Cool stuffing thoroughly. Stuffing is best made the day before roasting the goose.

ROAST TURKEY WITH CHESTNUT STUFFING

Turkey is the most popular bird for the Christmas feast today. The birds vary in quality (and price) from frozen to truly organic and free-range. If you are cooking a frozen bird you must allow sufficient time for it to thaw completely before cooking.

SERVES: Depending on size – allow at least 450 g/ 1lb per person

Ingredients:

1 turkey, drawn and plucked (defrosted fully if it has been frozen)

90 g/3 oz butter

salt and black pepper

For the chestnut stuffing:

450 g/1 lb whole, peeled chestnuts (vacuum-packed or tinned), roughly chopped

2 onions, peeled and finely chopped

the liver of the turkey, finely chopped or minced (optional)

450 g/1 lb good quality sausagemeat

30 g/1 oz butter

110 g/4 oz fresh breadcrumbs

1 heaped teasp paprika

1 egg, beaten

1 teasp fresh thyme, chopped

3 tablesp fresh parsley, chopped

a dash of wine or cider vinegar

For the giblet gravy:

the turkey giblets

1 onion, peeled and chopped

1 carrot, chopped

a few sprigs of thyme, a few stalks of parsley, a bay leaf, tied together with thread

salt and freshly ground black pepper

1 tablesp flour

125 ml/4 fl oz red wine

Method:

The giblet stock: Remove the liver and store in the fridge. Place the rest of the giblets, the onion, carrot and herbs in a pot. Cover with water, bring to simmering point, cover, and cook for about 45 minutes. Strain. Store in the fridge.

The chestnut stuffing: Melt the butter in a large pan and cook the onions gently until soft but not coloured. Set aside in a large mixing bowl. Add the chopped turkey liver to the pan and fry it gently, breaking it up with a spoon; when cooked add to the mixing bowl. Add the sausagemeat to the pan and spread it out as much as you can with a wooden spoon. Sprinkle with a little vinegar, this helps the meat to crumble and aids faster, even cooking. Cook the sausagemeat until lightly browned and cooked through. Add to the mixing bowl. Add the chestnuts, breadcrumbs, spices, herbs, and the egg to the mixing bowl. Mix well, season with black pepper (you are unlikely to need salt).

For food safety reasons it is not recommended that you stuff the cavity of the turkey. However, it's fine to stuff the neck end with some of this stuffing. The rest can be cooked, covered with foil, in a well-greased baking dish for about 40–60 minutes at the same temperature at which you cook the bird.

The turkey: If you are using a frozen turkey work out how long it will take to defrost. Defrosting should be done in a cool place and you should allow 24 hours for every 2–2.5 kg/4–5lb weight.

When fully defrosted and dried off inside, weigh the turkey and calculate the roasting time. Smear butter all over the breast and place a piece of foil loosely over the roasting tin (wrapping it tightly produces steamed, not roast, turkey).

Roast at 180°C/350°F/Gas 4 for 15 minutes per 450 g/1 lb plus another 15 minutes. You should also allow for 20–30 minutes resting time in a warm place. This allows the meat to settle, makes carving much easier, and gives you time to make the gravy, crisp up the roast potatoes, and glaze the ham (if it's for Christmas dinner).

You'll need to baste the bird at regular intervals, and in order to ensure a crisp brown skin remove the foil for the last 30 minutes of cooking. It is essential that all poultry is fully cooked. Use a skewer inserted into the thickest part of the thigh – the juices should run clear with no trace of pink. If the juices are not fully clear it needs more time in the oven.

The gravy: Pour off any excess fat from the roasting tin. Sprinkle about one tablespoon of flour over the base of the tin and stir over a low heat until it absorbs the remaining fat. Deglaze the pan with a glass of red wine, scraping all the crispy bits from the bottom of the tin and bubble up. Add the giblet stock and simmer, stirring until it's all amalgamated. Taste for seasoning and adjust if necessary. Pour into a hot gravy jug and keep warm.

ROAST SPATCHCOCKED CHICKEN WITH BREAD SAUCE

If you are lucky enough to find a real, organically fed, genuinely free-range chicken, by all means roast it in the conventional manner and you'll be in for a genuine taste of the past. For everyday supermarket chickens the method in this recipe has a number of advantages: you can pull off and discard all the loose fat and, because the chicken is cooked flat on a rack, all the watery juices escape and allow the skin to crisp in a satisfactory manner; the lemon and oil add flavour that mass-produced chickens lack.

SERVES 4

Ingredients:

1 chicken

the juice and rind of two lemons

2–3 tablesp olive oil

sea salt and crushed, or coarsely ground, black pepper

Method:

Using a poultry shears or strong scissors cut the chicken down each side of the backbone and remove this bone. Turn the chicken breast-side up and where the thighs meet the sides make a cut in the skin. Now press out the chicken flat. Turn over and where the legs meet the thigh make a cut in the skin and open the legs out flat too. Remove every visible sign of fat you can see and cut away excess skin at the neck end. Mix the lemon rind, lemon juice and pepper and about half the oil and marinate the chicken in this for 30 minutes.

Pre-heat the oven to 200°C/400°F/Gas 6. Set the flattened chicken on a rack, breast side down, for the first part of the cooking time – about 30 minutes. Turn it over, brush/baste with the juices and then brush with the remaining oil and sprinkle a little more pepper and sea salt lightly but evenly over the skin. Roast for a further 30–45 minutes or until the chicken is done through. The

Juices should run clear when pricked with a skewer in the thickest part of the thigh. Take up the chicken and allow it to rest.

Lovely eaten with salad and a loaf of real, crusty bread. Or, having cooked it this way, you can add all the traditional accompaniments like bread sauce (see below) and ham or crispy grilled rashers of bacon.

BREAD SAUCE

Ingredients:

60 g/2 oz breadcrumbs

300 ml/10 fl oz milk

1 small onion, peeled

5–6 whole cloves

salt and freshly ground white pepper

60 g/2 oz butter

2 shallots, peeled and very finely chopped

60 g/2 oz breadcrumbs

Method:

The trick with bread sauce is not to make it too far ahead of time. It does not take kindly to being kept waiting or being reheated. Stick the cloves in the onion. In a small pot bring the milk and onion to simmering point and then remove from the heat. Season with salt and pepper and allow to infuse for about an hour. Melt the butter in a small pan and gently fry the shallots until soft but not coloured. Remove the onion from the milk and pour the milk over the shallots. Add the breadcrumbs and heat very gently until hot through and thickened. If it is too thick just add more milk. Bread sauce should be well-seasoned so check it just before serving.

chicken Liver and Bacon Rolls

A tasy and economical starter (or snack) with a pleasing contrast in texture between the crisp bacon and the soft, juicy chicken livers.

SERVES 4 as a starter

Ingredients:

8 thinly-cut streaky rashers (of bacon)

8 chicken livers, cleaned and de-fatted

8 cocktail sticks, soaked in water

Worcestershire sauce

freshly ground black pepper

Method:

Remove the rinds from the bacon and use the blunt side of a knife blade to stretch the bacon slices out. Wash the livers and remove any fatty or tubular parts; dry on kitchen paper, then season with black pepper and a dash of Worcestershire sauce.

Roll a rasher around each liver and secure with a cocktail stick. Grill these rolls about 5 cm (2 inches) away from the heat. The idea is to brown and crisp the bacon while allowing the livers to be slightly pink and still juicy. Serve hot.

Duck Confit

A popular starter dish in Irish restaurants which is simple to make at home. All you need is some duck fat, which is easily collected by saving and clarifying the fat from a whole roast duck, or duck breasts which were roasted (if you want to confit a goose leg the same principle applies). Of course, you can confit any part of the duck but most people (and restaurants) prefer to keep the breasts for a quickly-cooked dish served pink and juicy.

SERVES 4

Ingredients:

4 duck legs

225 g/8 oz clarified duck fat

1 clove garlic, peeled and chopped

2 tablesp sea salt

1 tablesp sugar

1 sprig thyme, finely chopped

1 sprig rosemary, finely chopped

1 bay leaf, crumbled

Method:

Combine the garlic, sea salt, sugar, thyme, rosemary and bay leaf and rub this mixture into the duck legs. Place in a bowl, cover, and allow the flavours to develop in the fridge overnight. Take the duck legs from the bowl, rinse under cold running water and dry on kitchen paper. Preheat an oven to 120°C/250°F/Gas ½. Melt the duck fat over a gentle heat in a flameproof dish; add the duck legs and bring to a gentle simmer. Place in the oven and slow-cook for 1½–2 hours, or until the meat is very tender (falling off the bone). Remove from the oven and allow the legs to cool in the fat.

For immediate use, scrape off the duck fat (melt this later and filter through muslin and store for use with another confit, or for roasting potatoes). Heat a heavy pan, add a little oil and place the duck legs, skin side down, in the hot oil and cook until the skin is crisp.

Serve garnished with a seasonal salad (see over), with the emphasis on something crisp and fruity, as a contrast to the unctuous duck.

Salad suggestions:

Chopped apple and celery with a lemon and olive oil dressing.

Scallions sliced lengthways and ribbons of cucumber.

Watercress and peeled orange (sliced into segments); save the juice and whisk with a little light olive oil.

A simple combination of green salad leaves with some bitter ones like rocket, dandelion leaves, lambs lettuce, baby spinach, or chicory.

In winter this dish is good with braised red cabbage or stewed lentils.

ÐUCK BREASTS WITH FRESH RASPBERRY, ORANGE AND PORT SAUCE

Fruit sauces are traditional with duck. Raspberries are an indigenous Irish fruit that combine well with orange. The fruit sauce for this recipe can be made ahead of time, making this a quick and easy dish to prepare for guests.

SERVES 4

Ingredients:

4 duck breasts

salt and freshly ground black pepper

For the sauce:

125 ml/4 fl oz port

90 ml/3 fl oz water

1 tablesp sugar

225 g/8 oz fresh raspberries

the juice of two oranges

1 teasp cornflour or arrowroot

Method:

Make the sauce by placing the sugar, water and port in a small pot; bring to boiling point and stir until the sugar is dissolved; add most of the raspberries, keeping back a few to finish the sauce, and simmer very gently for about 5–6 minutes. Remove the seeds by puréeing the mixture in a hand-mill, or use the back of a wooden spoon to push the mixture through a fine-meshed sieve. Return the sauce to the pot and bring back to a fast simmer. Mix the cornflour or arrowroot with the orange juice, add a small amount of whole raspberries and add to the pot. Whisk as you bring the mixture back to the boil until it thickens slightly. Take off the heat and set aside until needed.

The trick with a quick-cooked duck breast served pink and juicy is to melt away as much of the fat beneath the skin as quickly as possible so the skin becomes crisp before the flesh is overcooked. With a razor-sharp knife make little criss-cross cuts in the skin. Heat a heavy pan and seal the breasts, skin-side down, over a high heat (don't use any oil or fat) for about three minutes until golden brown (wear gloves and long sleeves when you do this as the fat splattering from the duck can give you a nasty burn). Season with salt and black pepper. Remove from the pan and transfer to a rack set in a roasting tin and roast in a pre-heated oven at 220°C/425°F/Gas 7 for 8–10 minutes. Allow to rest in a warm place for a few minutes before slicing (skin side up) into a fan shape on a warm plate. Serve surrounded by the sauce.

Good accompanied by lightly-cooked snow (sugar) peas, mangetout, or runner beans.

CHICKEN BREASTS STUFFED WITH APPLES AND WHITE PUDDING, BAKED IN CIDER

Traditionally eaten for breakfast, white pudding is increasingly used as an ingredient. Here it adds a spicy taste to the stuffing and contrasts with the rich, but gently-flavoured cream and cider sauce.

SERVES 4

Ingredients:

4 breasts of chicken, complete with skin

90 g/3 oz open-textured white pudding, crumbled

1 cooking apple (Bramley), peeled, cored and finely chopped

60 g/2 oz fresh breadcrumbs

1 tablesp fresh parsley, chopped

1 tablesp chives, chopped

250 ml/8 fl oz medium dry Irish cider

90 ml/3 fl oz chicken stock

60 ml/2 fl oz double cream

salt and freshly ground black pepper

For the garnish:

2 red-skinned dessert apples, cored and sliced into thin wedges

Method:

Mix the white pudding, cooking apple, breadcrumbs, parsley and chives together and moisten with just a tablespoon or two of cider so that the mixture holds together. Partially lift the skin off the breasts and push equal amounts of the stuffing into the pockets formed.

Place the chicken breasts in one layer in a roasting tin just large enough to fit them snugly. Season the top with salt and freshly ground black pepper. Pour the cider and chicken stock around them and bake, covered, at 180°C/350°F/Gas 4 for 25–30 minutes. Uncover and continue cooking for a further 15–20 minutes until the chicken is cooked through and the skin crisply browned. Remove the chicken breasts and keep warm.

Add the cream to the pan juices and bring to boiling point, simmer until the liquid is reduced by half and the sauce is pleasingly thick. Check seasoning.

Serve the chicken surrounded by a little sauce, garnished with wedges of red-skinned dessert apples.

[You can substitute black pudding for the white pudding if you wish.]

QUAIL BRAISED WITH MUSHROOMS, WINE AND CREAM

A popular starter for a dinner party. Quails farmed by artisan food producers are a great favourite with chefs – one quail, one serving! They can be roasted, but even in their limited free-ranging life they can become tough. A slow-cooked quail has tender flesh and a delicate flavour. 'Wild' mushrooms are now grown in Ireland by artisan producers and even a small amount adds flavour and an interesting texture to the finished dish.

SERVES 4 as a starter or a light lunch

Ingredients:	For the braising:
4 quail	I onion, peeled and finely chopped
½ teasp juniper berries	I carrot, finely chopped
½ teasp black peppercorns	I sprig thyme
I teasp salt	120 g/4 oz fresh, farmed 'wild'
I clove garlic	mushrooms, sliced
8 thinly-cut bacon rashers	150 ml/5 fl oz white wine
I glass white wine or dry sherry	250 ml/8 fl oz crème fraîche
	a knob of butter
	I teasp olive oil

Method:

Mash the juniper berries, peppercorns, salt and garlic with a mortar and pestle. Stir in the wine or sherry and rub this mixture all over the skin of the quail. Wrap each bird in the rashers of thinly-cut bacon. Place in the fridge and allow to marinate overnight.

Heat the butter and oil in a pan, add the bacon-wrapped quails and brown lightly. Remove quails from the pan and place in an ovenproof casserole just large enough to fit them snugly. Add the onion and carrot to the pan and stir-fry until the onion softens. Add the mushrooms, thyme and wine, bubble up, then pour over the quails in the casserole. Cover and cook in the oven at 165°C/325°F/Gas 3 for about an hour, or until the quails are tender and cooked through. Remove the quails to rest in a warm place while you finish the sauce.

Add the crème fraîche to the casserole, stir over a very, very gentle heat until just hot through. Spoon a little of the mixture around each quail on a hot plate and serve at once.

Game

When the first hunter-gatherers arrived in Ireland they followed the migration of animals and fish. They, in turn, moved between campsites in an annual pattern governed by the seasonal migration of what they hunted or gathered. Native animals included wild boar (pig), which was their most important source of meat along with the native Irish hare and the native red deer. We know, too, from archaeological evidence that they hunted, trapped and ate pigeons, ducks, geese, red grouse, puffins and auks, along with other furred and feathered game that would never be eaten today. Successive waves of settlers brought new animals, especially the Normans who (unlike the native Irish who hunted only for food) were passionately fond of 'the chase', whether hawking for game birds, coursing hare, or hunting deer and wild boar. To supplement dwindling native stocks they introduced new birds and animals such as fallow deer, various game birds, the common hare and rabbits. The Normans also bred pigeons for the table, building elaborate dovecotes to house hundreds of birds. It became a kind of craze and strong Irish farmers, especially within The Pale (the Norman sphere of influence in Ireland), built smaller ones to hold perhaps a dozen birds. Today many ordinary Irish people breed pigeons – to race them!

A variety of game birds are available in Ireland, some common and some rare. Some are truly wild, but some are bred in captivity and then released into the wild for commercial shoots. The shooting seasons are strictly regulated and, by and large, the regulations are adhered to. Unlike some European countries, we do not shoot or eat small songbirds. The most common feathered game is pheasant, available fresh from November to January. This is also the season for less commonly available birds like the red-legged partridge, woodcock and snipe.

The season for wild ducks is longer: September to January. Mallard, teal and wigeon are the most available (and most popular) wild ducks. Our taste for wild goose has waned; perhaps because the flesh has a marked fishy taste or because the shooting season for it is so restricted – the Greylag may only be shot from 1 to 15 November, and the season for the Canada goose is from October to January. Farmers now consider wood pigeon a pest and shoot them all year round whenever they threaten crops (the official season is from June to January). One of the most prized game birds, the red grouse, is increasingly rare and may only be shot in September.

Being able to judge the age of a bird is important. Only young, tender birds respond well to roasting; older ones need slow cooking in liquid. It's not easy to tell if a bird is young but things to look out for include feet that are not too worn with scars or calluses. Try lifting the bird by the lower beak; the beak will snap if the bird is young. The breast should be soft and plump and the breastbone flexible. Feet are also the give-away with ducks and geese; when the birds are young the webbing between the toes tears easily.

Venison

Herds of wild deer roam the counties of Wicklow, Kerry and other upland areas. In some places they are now a pest, invading kitchen gardens and playing havoc with commercial crops. They are regularly culled (but the native red deer in the national park in County Kerry are protected). Wild deer has a wonderful flavour but it can be of uncertain age and may need tenderising and slow cooking. Farmed venison is always killed young and is always tender and tastes as good as the feed it is fed.

RABBIT STEW WITH BACON DUMPLINGS

Rabbits have passed into and out of favour since they were introduced by the Normans. In some areas they are a pest and difficult to keep out of gardens. Rabbits are also farmed commercially and young, tender rabbit makes a perfect small roast. The rabbit is still a wild animal, however, and those you might be presented with by sportsmen can be older and tougher. Then it is perfect for the classic Irish treatment – simmered until tender, then finished, browned and crisped in the oven. Rabbit stewed with cider or ale and bacon combines a number of Irish flavours to give a tasty winter dish.

SERVES 4

Ingredients:

1 rabbit (jointed)

1 onion

2 sticks celery

450 ml/15 fl oz ale or cider

30 g/1 oz butter

1–2 tablesp seasoned flour

For the dumplings:

110 g/4 oz rindless streaky bacon rashers

110 g/4 oz self-raising flour

1½ tablesp beef suet, grated

1 tablesp fresh chopped parsley

3 tablesp water

a pinch of salt

Method:

Peel the onion and chop it and the celery very finely. Stew these in the butter until soft. Remove them with a slotted spoon and fry the joints of rabbit (dusted in seasoned flour) in the butter remaining in the pan until they are browned on all sides. Place the rabbit with the onion and celery in a pot. Deglaze the frying pan with some of the ale or cider and add this to the pot with the rest of the ale or cider. Bring this to the boil quickly and then cover the pot and reduce the heat. Simmer for about 1–1½ hours until the rabbit is tender.

Make the dumplings by grilling the streaky bacon rashers until they are completely crisp. When they are cool chop them into a fine dice. Sift the flour and salt into a bowl and add the grated suet, chopped parsley and the diced bacon. Mix to a dough with the water. Shape into 8–10 little balls. Add them to the pan with the rabbit stew about 25–30 minutes before the end of cooking. They should be cooked through and well-risen. You could also make the dumplings with equal quantities of flour and cooked mashed potato.

ROAST HAUNCH OF VENISON

Deer meat is so lean that it usually needs to be 'larded' to prevent it drying out during roasting or grilling. It is also quite usual to marinate farmed venison for a day or two to add flavour.

SERVES 4–6

Ingredients:

1–1½ kg/2–3 lb haunch of venison

180 g/6 oz bacon or pork fat

110 g/4 oz fatty streaky bacon rashers or pork dripping

For the marinade:

250 ml/8 fl oz/1 cup wine vinegar or cider vinegar

500 ml/16 fl oz/2 cups dry white wine

250 ml/8 fl oz/1 cup olive oil

1 large onion, peeled and sliced

2 carrots, peeled and sliced

3 large sprigs parsley

3 sprigs fresh thyme

6 crushed black peppercorns

6 crushed juniper berries

1 teasp salt

Method:

Make sure the game dealer removes the outer membrane and draws the sinews from the haunch. Cut the bacon or pork fat into thin strips and use a larding needle to insert it into the haunch. When you have finished, the haunch should have the look of a bald, blunt hedgehog. Mix all the ingredients for the marinade in a large bowl and immerse the haunch completely. It needs at least 8–12 hours to marinate and if you are at all doubtful about the beast's age then give it 24–36 hours in a cool place. Turn the joint frequently in the marinade.

When you are ready to cook it, remove it from the marinade and dry it completely with kitchen paper. If using fatty streaky bacon, tie this around the joint so that at least the top is covered. If using pork dripping, render it down and paint the joint with about half of the fat. Roast in a pre-heated oven on a rack at 180°C/350°F/ Gas 4 for 20 minutes per 450g (1 lb) plus

20 minutes over. With regular basting with the remaining pork dripping, this should produce a joint still on the rare side (which is the way venison is served in Ireland). If you prefer it well-done, roast it for 30 minutes per 450 g (1 lb) plus 20 minutes more. If you have a joint which weighs more than 2 kg/4½ lb reduce the cooking time to 15 minutes per 450g (for rare) and no more than 25 minutes per 450g (for well done).

Allow the joint to rest for 10–15 minutes, then remove the fatty bacon and slice the venison thinly.

A traditional garnish is croutons (thinly sliced bread fried in a mixture of butter and olive oil until golden and crispy); seakale is a perfect vegetable accompaniment but celery is also acceptable and cabbage with juniper berries and garlic is also a favourite.

Serve the venison with the game sauce (below) and a dish of redcurrant or rowan jelly (see recipe, page 67).

GAME SAUCE

A very useful sauce to accompany a number of game dishes.

MAKES about 375 ml/12 fl oz

Ingredients:

1 tablesp finely chopped onion

1 tablesp finely chopped celery

2 tablesp good olive oil

1 tablesp flour

500 ml/16 fl oz good game or meat bone stock

1–2 tablesp rowan, or redcurrant, jelly

Method:

Heat the oil and gently sweat the vegetables in it until they are soft and just beginning to brown at the edges. Add the flour and cook until it is brown but not burnt. Add the stock to the pan and allow it to simmer for 40 minutes. Keep well stirred. Skim it, strain and return the thickened sauce to the pan with the rowan or redcurrant jelly. Stir over a gentle heat until the jelly has completely melted.

ROWAN JELLY

In Ireland the rowan tree is called the mountain ash. The Celts made wine from its bright scarlet berries and used them to flavour mead. It is a traditional accompaniment to venison and game birds. It used to be necessary to go up into the hills to collect the ripe berries but now you can see them in most suburban streets and gardens. I think I'd still be inclined to gather mine in the countryside, as far away from traffic fumes as possible!

MAKES 4–8 jars

Ingredients:

1.5 kg/3 lb ripe red rowan berries

900 g/2 lb cooking apples (crab apples if possible)

1 litre/ 32 fl oz water

450–900 g/1–2 lb sugar

Method:

Place the berries and the apples (washed but not peeled) in a pot with the water. Bring this to the boil and boil for about 40 minutes. Strain the contents of the pot overnight through a jelly bag. Measure the juice which passes through into the bowl. You will need 450 g/1 lb of sugar for each 500 ml/16 fl oz of juice. Boil the juice in a heavy-bottomed pot for 10 minutes, then add the correct amount of warmed sugar. Boil again for about 10 minutes more, skimming off any scum. Test for setting in the usual way and when the setting is right pour the jelly into sterilised jars and seal them at once. This jelly stores almost indefinitely (as long as the seal remains intact).

I use this method also to make a jelly from ripe elderberries, which I flavour with fresh, lightly bruised thyme leaves; these berries also have an affinity with game.

MARINATED FILLETS OF VENISON IN RED WINE AND PORT SAUCE

WITH A GRATIN OF CELERIAC, CREAM AND BACON

This recipe was created by Ross Lewis, chef and co-patron of Chapter One restaurant in Dublin, for an Irish Food Writers Guild awards luncheon, to show off the excellent quality of Moyallon venison

SERVES 4

Ingredients:

4 fillets of venison (450 g/1 lb)

110 g/4 oz butter

1 tablesp oil

For the marinade:

175 ml/6 fl oz ruby red port

175 ml/6 fl oz red wine

60 ml/2 fl oz olive oil

10 juniper berries

1 star anise

zest of one orange

1 sprig each of thyme and rosemary

5 black peppercorns, crushed

½ stick cinnamon

2 bay leaves

60 g/2 oz each of onion, celery, carrot and leek, finely chopped

sea salt and freshly ground black pepper

For the gratin:

1 head celeriac, peeled and thinly sliced

250 ml/8 fl oz cream

110 g/4 oz smoked bacon, finely chopped

Method:

Place all the marinade ingredients in a shallow non-metallic bowl. Add the venison, cover with cling film. Chill for at least one hour and up to six hours to allow the flavours to combine.

Place sliced celeriac in a 15 cm (6 inch) square roasting tin. Bring the cream and bacon to the boil in a pot and pour over the celeriac slices. Bake at 160°C/325°F/Gas 3 for about 20 minutes, pressing the slices down firmly (occasionally) during the cooking.

Remove the venison from the marinade; drain and pat dry with kitchen paper. Season fillets and allow to come to room temperature. Strain the marinade through a fine sieve into a pan and cook over a medium heat until reduced by two-thirds (slightly thickened and syrupy).

Heat a heavy-based pan and add the oil. Add the venison fillets and cook for 2–3 minutes. Turn over, add a knob of butter and cook for another minute or two, until medium rare but still pink in the centre. Remove from the heat and allow to rest for a couple of minutes.

Finish the sauce by re-heating and then whisking in the butter.

Divide the celeriac into four servings and arrange on a serving plate. Set the venison to one side and spoon the red wine sauce around. Serve with champ.

ROAST RED GROUSE WITH WILD BERRY SAUCE

It is sad that the native red grouse is such a rarity in Ireland today and that it is virtually impossible to get introduced birds (apart from the occasional brace) even in September. These are usually young birds and you will realistically need one for each person. This simple treatment can be used for other game birds like pheasant and various wild ducks like mallard, teal and wigeon. Only young birds are suitable for roasting. The method is the same but cooking times vary. As a rough guide, small game birds weighing up to 450 g/1 lb (like teal, pigeon, partridge) take 15–30 minutes total cooking time. Medium birds weighing from 500g–1kg like pheasant, mallard and wigeon are usually weighed and roasted for between 15–20 minutes per 450 g/1 lb weight depending on whether you like it cooked rare or well done. Large birds like a wild goose are roasted for 12–15 minutes per 450 g/1 lb. Small birds serve one person. In the medium-sized range you can, depending on size, get 2 servings.

SERVES 4

Ingredients:

2–4 grouse (depending on size and weight)

8 rashers of fatty streaky bacon

225 g/8 oz rowan berries, elderberries, fraughans, or cultivated redcurrants, or cranberries

2–3 tablesp water

1 teasp flour

250 ml/8 fl oz red wine

salt and black pepper

For the garnish:

4 slices toast or fried bread

4 small bunches of watercress, or lambs lettuce, or baby spinach leaves

Method:

Wipe out the cavity of the grouse and dry the skin well. Use the berries to stuff the cavity of each bird. Season the breast with salt and freshly ground black pepper. Tie the rashers of bacon over the breast of each bird with cotton string.

Roast at 230°C/450°F/Gas 8. The exact timing depends on the size of the bird. Most grouse will cook to the just barely pink stage in 20 minutes, a larger one will take 25 minutes. If you like them well-cooked add an extra five minutes. About half way through remove the bacon (which will be crisp) and keep warm. This allows the breast skin to crisp. Lift the birds from the roasting tin, draining off the berry juice from the cavity (add it to the gravy). Place on a warm serving platter and allow to rest for ten minutes in a warm place.

Make the gravy. Sprinkle a teaspoon of flour over the pan juices. Deglaze the pan with a little water, scraping all the crispy bits from the bottom of the tin. Add the wine and cooking juices and mix well. Strain into a small pot and allow to bubble up and concentrate. Strain into a hot sauce boat.

Place the grouse on pieces of crisp toast or fried bread with a bunch of watercress, lambs lettuce, or baby spinach. Serve with the piping hot sauce and a dish of rowan, elderberry or redcurrant jelly.

POT-ROASTED GAME BIRDS

Game birds past their first flush of youth are best cooked slowly. The Irish tradition was to cook them on a bed of vegetables in a large iron pot called a bastible; the older the bird, the longer it took to become tender. The vegetables are the usual pot herb mixture, onions and/or leek, carrot and celery, with thyme and parsley and a bay leaf. The liquid is a combination of game stock made with the trimmings and, sometimes, the legs of the birds and red wine, although there is a long tradition of using stout with pigeons.

The number of birds you need to make a main course for each person will depend on the birds chosen. As wild ducks come in various sizes it's best to consider the weight when working out how many you need. A duck weighing from 750–900g will serve two.

SERVES 4

Ingredients:

1–4 game birds

30 g/1 oz butter

1 onion

1 carrot

1 stick celery

1 leek (optional)

1 bunch of fresh herbs like thyme, bay leaf, parsley, tied together with string

2–8 rashers (slices) of fatty bacon

salt and freshly ground black pepper

150 ml/5 fl oz red wine

150 ml/5 fl oz game stock

For the stock:

giblets, hearts, neck, liver (and legs of smaller birds like pigeons – if using)

1 small onion, peeled and sliced

1 small carrot, peeled and sliced

500 ml/16 fl oz water

8 peppercorns

30 g/1 oz butter

600 ml/20 fl oz water

Method:

Clean the giblets and neck under running water and dry with kitchen paper. Melt the butter in a pot, add the giblets and vegetables and fry until the vegetables are soft and beginning to brown. Add the water, bay leaf and peppercorns. Bring to simmering point and cook at that heat for about one hour. Strain, cool and remove any fat that rises to the top.

Melt the butter in a large flame-proof and oven-proof casserole. Brown birds on all sides. Take up and set aside. Add the vegetables and fry for a few minutes until they begin to soften. Add the herbs and season with salt and black pepper. Lay the bacon over the breasts of the birds and set them on top of the vegetables. Pour in about half of the stock. Cover with a tightly fitting lid and simmer (or cook in a preheated oven at 165°C/325°F/Gas 3) until the birds are tender. Smaller, younger birds will take about three-quarters of an hour, older large ones up to one and a quarter hours.

Take up the birds and bacon and keep warm.

Finish the sauce. Add the wine to the casserole and bubble up, scraping the bottom of the pan to incorporate any crispy bits. Add the remaining stock and boil for a minute or two. You can serve the sauce with the chopped vegetables in it or, for a more elegant presentation, strain it to remove the cooked vegetables.

Small birds like quail are served whole. Medium-sized ones can be halved by cutting through the breast and then removing the back bone with a poultry shears. Serve on warm plates with a little of the sauce. This dish is served with roasted root vegetables, such as carrot, parsnips and turnip.

PIGEON BREASTS WITH ELDERBERRY SAUCE

Pigeons are plentiful and their dark meat is tasty. A double breast is the usual serving and that is how they are normally sold. Pigeons are rarely cooked whole. Even those who shoot and bring home their own pigeons usually just pluck the birds and slice off the breast fillets.

SERVES 4

Ingredients:

4 whole (double) pigeon breasts

1 tablesp oil

salt and freshly ground black pepper

½ a small onion, finely chopped

2–3 sprigs thyme

60 g/2 oz elderberries, stripped from stalk

125 ml/4 fl oz port

1 tablesp lemon juice

175 ml/6 fl oz game or poultry stock

30 g/1 oz butter

Method:

Season the breasts with salt and freshly ground black pepper. Heat oil in a pan, add the breasts and brown. Add the onion and thyme and a few tablespoons of the stock. Place in a baking dish. Cover. Cook in a preheated oven at 165°C/325°F/Gas 3 for about 45 minutes to one hour, or until tender and still juicy.

Simmer two-thirds of the elderberries in the stock, port, and lemon juice for about 10 minutes, reducing the amount of sauce by about a third. Strain through a fine mesh. Taste for seasoning and bring back to simmering point. Add the remaining elderberries and whisk in the butter. Serve with the pigeon breasts.

This sauce will go well with most game, particularly those in season in the autumn, when the elderberies are also in season and are widely eaten by game birds. Like all animals, game has an affinity to the food it eats.

spiced pears

A side dish for game birds. Pears come into season at the same time as the game season begins and this sweet/sour garnish works well with many game birds.

SERVES 4 as a garnish or side dish

Ingredients:

2 fairly firm pears
(old-fashioned cooking
pears work well)

125 ml/4 fl oz water

125 ml/4 fl oz wine vinegar

110 g/4 oz sugar

2 teasp cloves

¼ teasp nutmeg, grated

2 cm (1 inch) of stick
cinammon

salt and freshly ground black
pepper

Method:

Peel and halve the pears and remove as many of the seeds as you can. Place all the ingredients in a pot just large enough to hold the pears. Simmer until the pears are just tender but still firm. Cool.

GAME PIE

A raised game pie came from the 'big house' tradition where a surfeit of game needed to be used up. Its substantial crust allowed it to be transported to the next day's shoot. Today you are more likely to encounter a game terrine, which serves the same purpose of recycling bits and bobs of leftover game and, by good fortune, the way you make the pie filling is the same. So the choice is yours, pie or terrine. What went into a game pie depended on what leftover game was available (and the mood of the cook). The filling is made up of a forcemeat (minced pork, bacon and fat), mixed game and a jelly made from game stock or pig's trotters.

SERVES 6–8 as a main course

Ingredients:

For the forcemeat:

700 g/1½ lb pork, chopped

200 g/7 oz bacon, chopped

100 g/3½ oz hard pork fat, chopped

3–4 leaves of fresh sage, finely chopped

2 teasp anchovy essence

a pinch each of cloves, nutmeg, cinnamon and freshly ground black pepper

For the game filling:

900 g/2 lb game meat as available, boned and all skin removed

For the hot water crust pastry:

450 g/1 lb strong white flour

175 g/6 oz lard

150 ml/5 fl oz hot water

½ teasp salt

For the jelly:

300 ml/10 fl oz game or meat stock

15 g/½ oz gelatine

Method:

Mince, or chop briefly in a food processor, the pork, bacon and fat to make the forcemeat. Mix in the seasonings, the anchovy essence and sage. Fry a little of the mixture until done through, cool, and taste the seasoning; adjust as you feel necessary. Set aside.

A good mix of game will give the best result, especially if you have a mixture of furred and feathered. If you have only leftover pheasant you can always add colour and interest to the flavour with a few pigeon breasts, or a small wild duck, or some rabbit. If you have a lot of venison you can use some chicken or domestic duck and rabbit to balance the strong flavour. Check that all skin and bones are removed and cut the game into neat pieces. Set aside.

Make the pie crust. Lightly grease a raised pie mould, or a loose-bottomed or spring-form cake tin about 21–22½ cm (8–9 inches) in diameter. Sift flour and salt into a bowl. Make a well in the centre. Bring lard and water to the boil and simmer for a few minutes. Pour the mixture into the centre of the flour, mixing well with a spoon, until it is cool enough to handle. Knead well, keeping it as warm as possible. Leave it to relax in a warm place for 30 minutes and then knead again. Reserve about one quarter for the lid. Roll out the remaining pastry to fit the mould or tin, raising the sides above the level of the tin. Roll out the top and place on greaseproof paper.

Place half the forcemeat mixture on the bottom of the moulded pastry. Lay the game pieces on top, mounding them up slightly. Finish with the rest of the forcemeat mixture. Fit the pastry lid on top, pressing the edges of the top and bottom so that it is well sealed. Cut a hole in the top to allow steam to escape. The hole should be large enough to fit a small funnel, through which you will later pour the jelly. Brush the top with beaten egg.

Place in a roasting tin and bake in an oven preheated to 190°C/375°F/Gas 5 for 15 minutes. Then reduce the temperature to 150°C/300°F/Gas 2 and bake for a further 1¾ hours. Cool and place in the fridge overnight.

The next day sprinkle the gelatine over the stock. Soak for five minutes. Bring slowly to the boil and simmer for a minute or two. Leave it to get cold but not set; it should be syrupy. Insert a small funnel in the hole in the lid of the pie and pour in the jelly, a little at a time. Continue until you can just see the level of liquid within the pie. Keep a sharp eye out to check that the jelly is not leaking through any holes in the pastry. If it is, stop pouring, plug the holes with a little softened butter and replace the pie in the fridge until the butter is set firm. Then pour in the rest of the jelly. Chill the pie for about 2 hours until the liquid is set.

GAME TERRINE

Converting the previous recipe for Game Pie into a game terrine is simplicity itself. This amount will fill two x 1–1½ litre/2–3 pint terrines.

SERVES 12–16 as a starter

Ingredients:

Game filling, forcemeat and jelly ingredients as in Game Pie recipe

thin slices of pork fat, or slices of unsmoked streaky bacon with rinds removed

Method:

Line a terrine with the slices of pork or bacon. Fill as for the pie. Cover with more slices of pork fat or bacon. Cover and set the terrine in a roasting tin half-filled with hot water. Bake at 180°C/°F350f/Gas 4 for about 1–1½ hours. Cool and when almost fully cold remove the cover and pour in the jelly. Cool for at least two hours before using (better still, refrigerate overnight to allow the flavours to develop).

Smoked, cured and spiced meats

Curing foods with salt grew out of the need to preserve shoaling summer fish, like herring and mackerel, and grass-fed animals which were usually killed at the beginning of winter. The salt was extracted from seaweed.

The Irish tradition of smoking food (like that of many northern European countries) was dictated by the damp, humid climate which made air-drying of fish (even small ones) difficult and meat all but impossible. Oak and beech grew in our woodlands and these were burned to smoke foods. Need turned into love and from ancient times to this day the Irish have salt-cured or smoked pretty well anything. Since the fourteenth century, Ireland has exported cured and smoked fish and corned beef (salted beef) in vast quantities. Brisket was the traditional cut for corned beef but today the leaner silverside and topside cuts are more popular. They are cooked slowly in water with pot herbs, stout or cider, and are traditionally eaten with cabbage. Spiced beef is extremely popular at Christmas. Dry-spicing was the traditional cure but today wet-spicing is more common.

Bacon and ham are eaten smoked but also 'pale' (cured but unsmoked). Each type is so popular that Irish shops always offer both. Craft butchers and artisan producers use natural woods for smoking: oak or beech, or a mixture. So great is the Irish love of smoked foods that in recent times artisan producers have expanded the range of meats they smoke; the list now includes lamb, pork, duck, chicken and speciality sausages.

While some pork was eaten fresh, most of it it was salted (cured) to make it last. When a pig was slaughtered, it was bled, cleaned and the carcass split lengthways from tail to snout. Sometimes the head was detached in one piece (the cheeks were a particular delicacy) lightly brined and then used to make brawn (potted head cheese). The fillets were always removed and eaten fresh along with the kidneys, heart, liver, brain and sweetbreads, stomach and intestine (kept as casing for puddings and sausages), the feet and tail were usually lightly brined. The hams were often treated separately for curing (or for roasting uncured in wealthier establishments). What remained was two 'flitches' for curing as bacon. They were usually, but not exclusively, dry-cured, by rubbing with a mixture of salt, sugar and saltpetre (over a period as long as two weeks). They were then dried, and often smoked over a mixture of juniper berries, turf and oak. Today, real dry-cured bacon is hard to come by. Most bacon is now processed in large factories, wet-cured in brine and 'smoked' (dyed) by various chemical means. Some pork butchers working in the traditional way survive, and when you find one, treasure him!

Guilds of craftsmen and tradesmen have existed in Ireland since medieval times and, along with twenty-eight other guilds, the butchers took part in the annual performances of the medieval Mystery Play cycles. The butchers always represented the 'tormentors of Christ with their garments well and truly peinted'. The Irish Craft Butchers Association, which represents traditional family butchers, still runs a mumber of annual competitions to find the All-Ireland champion in pudding-making, sausage-making, spiced beef preparation and speciality meat products. It is heartening to see how many young butchers take part. Not only do they carry on old traditional methods but they respond to their creative instincts and often develop innovative products that enhance the reputation of Irish meat and poultry. There is also a welcome trend (small but growing) for farmers to work closely with smaller butchers to supply the butchers and sell direct to the public at farmers' markets.

BACON AND CABBAGE

Traditionally the cabbage was washed, sliced and added to the pot in which the bacon was cooking, often for an hour or more, but the modern taste for vegetables which are not 'murdered' in this way dictates that it is now more usual to take a cup of the liquid from the bacon pot and bring it back to the boil in a separate pot to which the finely-shredded cabbage is added and cooked very quickly until just tender.

SERVES 4–6

Ingredients:

1 joint of bacon (shoulder, collar, or streaky cut from the belly)

1 onion, peeled

1 carrot

1 stalk celery

1 bay leaf

6–8 dried juniper berries

some parsley stalks

1 teasp sugar (optional)

a generous dash of wine vinegar (optional)

1 large green cabbage (York or Sweetheart are the favourites), tough stalks removed, then finely shredded

Method:

Modern bacon tends toward low-salt cures, but if you feel it may be too salty you should soak the joint overnight in several changes of cold water. It is then brought to the boil for 5 minutes in the final change of water, which is discarded.

The joint is then put into a pot of fresh water along with the pot herbs – onion, celery, carrot, a bay leaf or two (parsley stalks, juniper berries, a dollop of sugar and a dash of wine vinegar are all common additions). Bring to the boil and then reduce the heat immediately to a bare simmer. Cook for 25–30 minutes per 450 g/1 lb. It should be very tender. If the whole joint is to be eaten hot, remove the skin and slice the bacon quite thickly. As well as the cooked cabbage, a white parsley sauce and floury boiled or steamed potatoes (in their skins) are the traditional accompaniments.

If part of the joint is to be kept for another meal the skin is left on and that meat is put back into its cooking liquid to cool naturally. This keeps it moist and makes it much tastier as a cold cut.

BAKED HAM WITH CIDER, MUSTARD & APPLE SAUCE

This is a rather more aristocratic dish because hams were the prime cuts of the pig. They were usually lightly brined and then smoked. There are a variety of ways of doing this but the most famous, Limerick Ham, was smoked using juniper berries. Oak shavings were often used. An eighteenth-century recipe adds an unusual ingredient: 'Hang in a chimney and make a fire of oak shavings and lay over it horse litter and one pound of juniper berries. Keep the fire smothered down for two or three days and then hang them to dry.'

SERVES 4–6

Ingredients:	12 whole cloves
1 joint of ham	250 ml/8 fl oz/1 cup freshly squeezed orange juice
1 onion, peeled	
1 carrot	For the sauce:
1 celery stalk	
1 bay leaf	1 Bramley cooking apple, peeled, cored and chopped
8 whole black peppercorns	
For the glaze:	300 ml/10 fl oz cider
	1 teasp sugar, or to taste
2–3 tablesp Demerara sugar	1 tablesp wholegrain Irish mustard
1 teasp English mustard powder	2 teasp butter

Method:

Soak the joint for 12 hours in two changes of water. Place in a large pot, add vegetables, bay leaf and peppercorns and cover with cold water. Bring slowly

to simmering point, cover and barely simmer for 25 minutes for each 450 g/
1 lb (for joints over 3.5 kg/8 lb, allow 20 minutes per 450 g/1 lb). Leave to
cool a little in its cooking liquid off the heat.

Lift out and remove the skin, leaving the fat. Mix the sugar and dry mustard
powder and press evenly all over the joint. With a sharp knife cut a lattice
pattern in the fat. Press back any coating that falls off. Stick a clove into the
cuts where the lines cross. Heat oven to
220°C/425°F/Gas 7. Place the
ham in a roasting tin
surrounded by the
orange juice.

Bake for about 20
minutes or until the
sugar has slightly
caramelised.

Cook the apple in the
cider and sugar until soft.
Beat with a wooden spoon
until smooth. Stir in the
mustard and butter and season
to taste.

Baked ham is often served cold with a variety of salads.

CORNED BEEF

Corned beef is mentioned in the eleventh-century dream poem, Aislinge Meic Con Gline:
'Many wonderful provisions, Pieces of palatable food
Full without fault, Perpetual joints of corned beef.'

SERVES 4–6

Ingredients:

1¼ kg/3 lb (approx) corned beef (silverside, topside, round, rump **or** brisket, which is much fattier)

1 onion, peeled

1 carrot

bouquet garni

2 cloves garlic

some parsley stalks

500 ml/1 pt/2 cups/ (small bottle) dry cider

Method:

Soak the meat overnight in several changes of water. Place all the ingredients in a large ovenproof pot with fresh water to cover. Bring to the boil, skimming all the while. Reduce heat to a bare simmer and cover tightly. Cooked in the oven at 150°C/ 300°F/ Gas 2, it takes between 40 to 60 minutes per 450 g/1 lb. Tenderness varies (depending on beast, cut and cure), so test when three-quarters of the cooking time has elapsed.

If you intend to eat the meat cold, as many Irish prefer, allow it to cool in the cooking water, then remove to a plate and press lightly, either in a meat press or by covering with a plate weighed down by 2 x 400g foodtins.

Traditionally, when eaten hot, corned beef is served with colcannon and a simple white parsley sauce or a mustard sauce.

Cold, it is served with brown soda bread and traditional salad leaves and chutnies.

spiced beef

Spices have been imported into Ireland since earliest times, but were always scarce and expensive, so this dish was one reserved for a festive feast, particularly at Christmas. It's a tradition that lives on today and no Christmas cold table is complete without it. Dry-spicing is the older, more interesting way of curing it, but it has to be said, wet spicing has its fans – some people even defend the modern butchers' method of 'spicing-up' corned beef which, although good to eat if you choose your butcher carefully, is not really the same at all. Do weigh the ingredients for this recipe carefully.

SERVES 6–10

Ingredients for Spicing:	Ingredients for Cooking:
about 2 kg/4½ lb beef (silverside, topside, round, rump, **or** brisket)	bunch of thyme
15 g/½ oz saltpetre	bay leaves
225 g/8 oz sea salt	1 onion, studded with cloves
30 g/1 oz allspice	1 carrot
30 g/1 oz whole black peppercorns	1 stick celery
90 g/3 oz dark brown sugar	12 whole peppercorns
12 dried juniper berries (crushed)	
a big pinch of ground cloves	
2 bay leaves	

Method:

Mix the salt and saltpetre and rub some of it into the meat, making sure it gets well into all the hollows and cracks. Place in a glass or other non-metal bowl and keep covered in the fridge or another really cool place. Repeat this procedure every day for 4 days. Then grind the whole spices and mix them with the sugar, cloves and bay leaves. Rub this mixture into the beef and place in a clean dish. Store in the fridge. Every second day for 10–14 days, turn the joint over and rub in the spices that adhere to the meat.

To Cook:

Tie a bunch of thyme and a few bay leaves to the joint. Place it in a pot just large enough to fit the meat. Add an onion stuck with a few cloves, a carrot, a stick of celery and a dozen whole peppercorns. Cover with cold water (mixed, if you wish, with a bottle of stout, for a distinctive flavour). Bring to simmering point, cover tightly and cook in a low oven set to 140°C/275°F/ Gas 1 for about 5 hours. If you prefer, simmer it gently for about 3½ hours on the hob. It should be quite soft and tender when fully cooked.

Spiced beef can be eaten hot but it is more usual to serve it cold. To do this, allow it to cool in the cooking liquid for about 2 hours, then remove it, wrap in greaseproof paper and press it lightly while stored in the fridge. Slice very thinly with a very sharp knife. It is often served as finger food on brown bread spread with a fruit chutney, with chopped pickles (sweet and sour pears, sweet pickled onions, or piccalilli are good), or as a plated dish with a green salad, or a celery and walnut salad, and crusty white bread and butter.

oak-smoked lamb with oven-dried tomatoes and mint with a leek mash

Oak-smoked lamb is a contemporary creation that recently won an Irish Food Writers Guild Good Food Award for Pat Doherty of Doherty's Family Butchers in Enniskillen, County Tyrone. Pat is a young craft butcher with a creative instinct and skills to match. The intense and slightly sweet flavour of oven-dried tomatoes contrasts well with the lightly-smoked Irish lamb. The recipe was created by Derry Clarke of L'Écrivain restaurant in Dublin for the awards luncheon.

SERVES 4

Ingredients:

4 oak-smoked lamb steaks

For the tomatoes:

½ tablesp butter

½ tablesp olive oil

2 large ripe plum tomatoes, halved

2 tablesp balsamic vinegar

2 tablesp extra virgin olive oil

2 cloves garlic, sliced

2 teasp fresh mint, chopped

sea salt and freshly ground black pepper

For the leek mash:

900 g/2 lb floury potatoes, cooked and mashed while still hot

450 g/1 lb leeks, trimmed, sliced

3–4 tablesp fresh parsley, chopped

butter, to taste

Method:

Place the tomato halves on a wire rack, skin side down. Brush with olive oil and balsamic vinegar; place a slice of garlic on each one; sprinkle the mint on top and season with sea salt and black pepper. Place in an oven set to

80°C/200°F/Gas ¼ for about two hours. The finished tomatoes should be dried out but not leathery.

Lamb steaks are usually cut thinly and are best eaten while still pink and juicy within. Fry on a ridged grill or under a very hot grill for about two minutes on each side or until done to your taste. Season after cooking with black pepper and a sprinkle of sea salt and rest for a minute or two before serving.

Slice the leeks into thin diagonal strips, drop into boiling water and simmer for five minutes. Drain and mix immediately into the hot mashed potato and beat until well mixed. Add butter and parsley. Season with salt and black pepper and mix again. Serve hot.

WARM BLACK PUDDING AND CARAMELISED APPLE SALAD

Black pudding, often teamed with apples, is a popular starter in restaurants. It also makes a great dish for a light luncheon.

SERVES 4–6 as a starter

Ingredients:

450 g/1 lb black pudding

2 large, firm eating apples

90 g/3 fl oz runny honey

175 ml/6 fl oz balsamic vinegar

olive oil to taste

mixed salad leaves

Method:

Pre-heat oven to 180°C/350°F/Gas 4. Slice pudding into rounds about 2.5 cm (1 inch) thick. Place on a non-stick baking sheet. Core and peel the apples and divide into six pieces. Cook these with the honey in a heavy ovenproof pan until caramelised. Add the vinegar and place in the oven for a further five minutes. Take the apples from the pan, reserving the juice, and position around heated serving plates.

For the salad dressing, quickly mix the reserved pan juices with olive oil to taste, season with a little salt and black pepper and whisk.

Place salad leaves in the centre of the plate and drizzle over a little dressing. Place black pudding on top and serve at once with a little wholemeal bread.

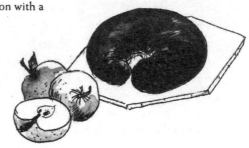

WARM BACON SALAD WITH WILTED LEAVES

Made from readily available ingredients, this fast and simple dish makes a flavoursome starter or a light lunch.

SERVES 4 as a starter

Ingredients:

110–175 g/4–6 oz mixed salad leaves

225 g/8 oz thickly-sliced rashers of streaky bacon (preferably dry-cured), rind removed

1 tablesp olive oil

2–3 tablesp cider vinegar

freshly ground black pepper

shavings of Irish Gabriel or Desmond cheese from West Cork (or parmesan), optional

Method:

Assemble a mixture of slightly bitter salad leaves like rocket, frisée (curly endive), baby spinach, lambs lettuce, dandelion leaves and watercress. Wash and dry the leaves and place on serving plates.

Cut bacon into matchsticks. Heat a tablespoon of oil in a pan and cook the bacon pieces, turning frequently – the idea is to get the fat to run and the bacon to become lightly brown and crisp. Take pan from the heat and remove bacon on to kitchen paper. You are aiming to have about 3–4 tablespoons of bacon fat remaining, if there is too much, discard some. Add the vinegar and deglaze the pan by stirring vigorously and scraping up any crispy bits in the pan. The residual heat should concentrate the vinegar so that it reduces by about half. Use the contents of the pan to dress the leaves, tossing them to coat; the hot dressing will wilt them slightly. Sprinkle bacon over the top with shavings of cheese and eat at once. It's rather good with fresh white soda bread to mop up the juices.

TRADITIONAL CORK CRUBEENS

This wonderful traditional recipe comes from Declan Ryan, formerly chef/co-owner of The Arbutus Hotel in Cork, a place long renowned for fine food. In recent years Declan has transformed himself into an artisan baker and now makes the award-winning Arbutus breads. Hind feet are preferred because they have more meat on them (the less-favoured front feet are called trotters). Crubeens are eaten with your fingers, accompanied by Irish soda bread and washed down by stout.

SERVES 4

Ingredients: For the brine (will cure at least 4–8 crubeens):

10 litres/1 gallon water

225 ml/8 fl oz honey

200 g/7 oz brown sugar

1 cinnamon stick

4 bay leaves

400 g/ 14 oz coarse salt

For the crubeens:

4 crubeens (pigs' hind feet)

2 carrots, chopped

1 stick celery, chopped

1 onion, chopped

250 ml/8 fl oz white wine vinegar

110 g/4 oz butter

400 g/14 oz dried breadcrumbs

¼ teasp allspice

Method:

Mix the brine ingredients together and soak crubeens in this for 48 hours. Remove from the brine and tie each pair (2) crubeens together on to a wooden dowel. This helps them keep their shape as they cook. Put into a large stock or ham pot and add the vegetables. Add vinegar and cover with water. Simmer for 6–7 hours over a gentle heat. Take the pot off the heat and allow to cool fully. Carefully lift out the double crubeen packs, remove string and dowel.

Melt the butter and mix with the dried breadcrumbs and allspice. Coat the crubeens with this. Warm the crubeens, either under a grill set at a low heat or in an oven set to 160°C/325°F/Gas 3. Cook until hot through inside and the coating is crisp and golden. Enjoy! Just guzzle and forget about the implications.

ROAST KASSELER WITH APPLE SAUCE AND ROAST POTATOES

This cured and lightly-smoked pork was brought to Ireland at the beginning of the twentieth century by a number of German family pork butchers and when correctly made is highly prized. Only prime cuts of pork loin (sometimes with the fillet) are lightly brined, then briefly smoked. Kasseler makes a wonderful Sunday roast but is also very good cold, served thinly-sliced, with a traditional fruit chutney.

SERVES 4–6

Ingredients:

1.4 kg/3 lb loin of kasseler

900 g/2 lb floury potatoes, peeled and halved (if large)

2 large cooking apples (preferably Bramley), peeled and cored

3 tablesp water

1 tablesp butter

sugar to taste

a little freshly ground black pepper

Method:

Score the fat of the joint in a diamond pattern. Place on a rack in a roasting tin, fat side up (the crisp fat of kasseler is one of the joys of eating it). Roast at 165°C/325°F/Gas 3 for about 20 minutes per 450g/ 1 lb and until the fat is brown and crisp on top. As soon as the fat starts to run, drain it off into a second roasting tin and use it to roast potatoes. Place this tin in the oven until the fat is very hot. Add the potatoes and turn unitl coated on all sides. Roast, turning at least once, at the same heat as the kasseler for approx one hour, or until soft and tender on the inside and golden and crisp on the outside. Meanwhile make the apple sauce. Place apples and water in a pot; cover and cook over a medium heat until soft. Good cooking apples will turn into a fluffy mass if lightly beaten with a fork. Stir in the butter and add sugar to taste. Serve hot with the kasseler.

Ready-to-eat, smoked, air-dried meats, poultry, or game birds

Driven by artisan producers and very much in tune with Irish tastes, there is now a range of ready-to-eat smoked and cured meats, poultry and game available. Needless to say, chefs love using them as quickly prepared and popular starters. They are normally served thinly-sliced with a little salad, salsa, fruity or pickled accompaniments, and sometimes a combination of all three!

The recipes here contrast the smokiness with a slightly sweet flavour, but they could equally well be served with a mixed leaf salad or a fruity salsa.

Smoked duck with beetroot and orange

SERVES 4 as a starter

Ingredients:

175–225 g/6–8 oz smoked duck, thinly sliced

juice of 1 orange

1 teasp grated orange zest

4 leaves of crisp cos lettuce (or other crisp leaves)

425 g/1 lb beetroot

Method:

Vacuum-packed, cooked peeled beetroot works fine for this dish. Otherwise choose small young beetroots and bake without peeling until tender (1–1½ hours). Wearing gloves (unless you want to dye your hands pink), peel the cooked beets thinly and cut into large cubes. Dress with orange juice. Place a crisp lettuce leaf on each plate, divide the cubed beetroot between each leaf and sprinkle a little orange zest over the top. Serve with the smoked duck.

AIR-DRIED CONNEMARA LAMB WITH WILD IRISH SALAD

We have no tradition of air-dried foods. The rather wet and often humid Irish climate prevented this form of preserving being used in the past. Modern techniques in controlling air temperature and moisture levels have encouraged creative young craft butchers to experiment with air-drying Irish lamb, beef and pork, with some wonderful results. Leading restaurants now feature air-dried meat on starter or charcuterie trollies and buffets. It's usually simply served with a mixed leaf salad, allowing the excellent flavour of the meat to speak for itself.

SERVES 4 as a starter

Ingredients:

225 g/8 oz air-dried Connemara lamb, thinly sliced

For a 'strange', wild Irish salad:

wild leaves

1 tablesp lemon juice or cider vinegar

3–4 tablesp olive oil

a little sea salt and freshly ground black pepper

Method:

'The cress are on the water and the sorrels are at hand'. This line of poetry, translated by Sir Samuel Ferguson from the Irish, gives a clue to some of the leaves commonly eaten by the native Irish. 'Strange' salads are often mentioned in old accounts of the Irish way with salads. Fortunately, many of the leaves and flowers grow wild so that what you choose is limited only by seasonal availability and individual preference. Select from the following: wild sorrel, watercress, wild garlic leaves (ramsoms), dandelion leaves, young beech leaves, hawthorn leaves, lambs lettuce, comphrey, chickweed, wild mint, thyme, marjoram, primrose flowers, borage flowers, nasturtium flowers. Bring the lamb to room temperature while you prepare the salad, dressing it at the last second by tossing the leaves lightly in the dressing.

smokeᎠ chickeᎱ or quail with ribbons of sweet pickleᎠ cucumber

The gentle sweet/sour flavour of the cucumber is a perfect foil to smoked chicken or quail. Smoked poultry is ready-to-eat and popular as a simply prepared starter or light lunch.

SERVES 4 as a starter

Ingredients:

175–225 g/6–8 oz smoked chicken or quail, thinly sliced

1 cucumber, about 310 g/ 10 oz

150 ml/5 fl oz white wine vinegar

150 g/5 oz sugar

1 teasp fennel seeds

salt and freshly ground black pepper

Method:

Combine the vinegar, sugar and fennel seeds in a pot. Bring to the boil and cook only until the sugar dissolves. Cool and season to taste. Wash, top and tail the cucumber, and slice lengthways in very thin ribbons. Place in a flat-ish dish. Pour the liquid over the cucumber and allow to marinate, covered, in the fridge for at least 30 minutes. Drain very well and serve as a garnish for the smoked chicken.